MANAGING A SUCCESSFUL INTERNATIONAL ADMISSIONS OFFICE

NAFSA's Guide to International Admissions

MANAGING A SUCCESSFUL INTERNATIONAL ADMISSIONS OFFICE

NAFSA's Guide to International Admissions

EDITED BY David L. Di Maria

Edited by David L. Di Maria

NAFSA: Association of International Educators
1307 New York Avenue, NW
8th Floor
Washington, DC 20005-4715

NAFSA is the largest association of professionals committed exclusively to advancing international higher education. The association provides leadership to its diverse constituencies through establishing principles of good practice and providing professional development opportunities. NAFSA encourages networking among professionals, convenes conferences and collaborative dialogues, and promotes research and knowledge creation to strengthen and serve the field. We lead the way in advocating for a better world through international education.

Library of Congress Cataloging-in-Publication Data

Names: Di Maria, David L., 1981- editor. | NAFSA: Association of International Educators (Washington, DC)
Title: Managing a successful international admissions office: NAFSA's guide to international admissions / edited by David L. Di Maria.
Description: First Edition. | Washington, DC: NAFSA: Association of International Educators, [2017] | Includes index.
Identifiers: LCCN 2017010967 (print) | LCCN 2017017800 (ebook) | ISBN 9781942719090 (Kindle) | ISBN 9781942719106 (iBook) | ISBN 9781942719151 (Universal/Android) | ISBN 9781942719083 (pbk.)
Subjects: LCSH: Students, Foreign—United States. | Universities and colleges—United States—Admission.
Classification: LCC LB2376.4 (ebook) | LCC LB2376.4 .M36 2017 (print) | DDC 378.1/982691—dc23 LC record available at https://lccn.loc.gov/2017010967

Edited by Lisa Schock, NAFSA

First edition, 2017

10 9 8 7 6 5 4 3 2 1

For my wife, Masha, and my son, Charlie.

Contents

Acknowledgments

This book began as an idea born out of necessity.

In 2014, I accepted the newly established position of associate provost for international programs at Montana State University. One of my first major initiatives was to streamline international admissions by consolidating processes within the Office of International Programs.

Over a period of several months, I worked diligently with internal and external stakeholders to map the current admissions workflow, update administrative systems, and assist my staff to develop expertise related to international admissions given that their responsibilities for international enrollment management (IEM) had mostly been limited to recruitment.

As I began to compile training resources for my IEM team, it was not long before I realized that while there existed an extensive body of literature related to international student recruitment, comprehensive publications focused on international admissions were few and far between. My office's newly established IEM reference library had an empty place on its bookshelf, and it became my goal to fill this void.

NAFSA is an amazing professional association and one of the reasons for that is its incredible staff. I want to thank Joann Ng Hartmann, Martha Hawley-Bertsch, Cody Jameson, Lisa Schock, Sheila Schulte, and Leslie Taylor for believing in this project and for believing in me. I also wish to acknowledge the work of Kathleen Dyson, the designer of the book's cover. She turned an abstract concept of multidimensional systems thinking into art.

In closing, I thank the authors for their willingness to share their expertise and experiences in written form, the NAFSA members who agreed to review the book and provide feedback prior to its publication, and you, the reader, for your interest in the highly nuanced, dynamic, and exciting world of IEM.

David L. Di Maria

1 Introduction to International Enrollment Management

By David L. Di Maria

As a professional domain, international enrollment management (IEM) is concerned with the international student experience—from prospect to alumni. Yet the majority of IEM publications focus exclusively on international student recruitment or international student services. Aside from technical resources specifically developed to assist with the evaluation of foreign academic credentials, there is very little information currently available within the professional literature to guide faculty, staff, and others through the nuances, considerations, and baseline practices of international admissions.

This book fills that void by providing a comprehensive overview of issues related to international admissions. Each of the chapters is written from the perspective of a single practitioner and the content is presented in a general way so as to be applicable across institutional types. It is our aim that this book will serve as a resource for a wide audience including guidance counselors, international admissions staff, faculty, and senior administrators interested in increasing the efficiency of their admissions processes while also improving the international student experience.

A Systems Approach to IEM

IEM is a unique branch of enrollment management. Depending upon the institution, IEM may fall entirely or partially under the purview of the chief enrollment officer or it may be assigned to an entirely different division, such as academic affairs. Regardless of how IEM fits within an institution's

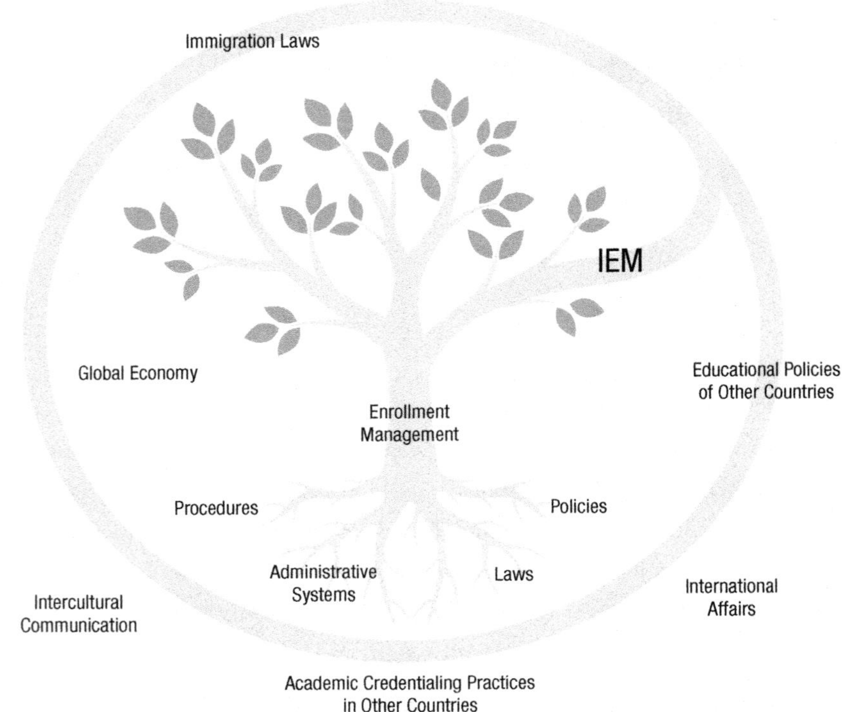

organizational structure, it is increasingly recognized as a critical component of overall enrollment plans, internationalization strategies, and twenty-first-century diversity initiatives.

Staff members responsible for IEM must generally understand the same laws and regulations, policies and procedures, and administrative systems that influence the work of their colleagues working in domestic enrollment management, but they must also maintain additional areas of expertise including immigration law, educational policies of countries other than the one in which they work, and academic credentialing practices used around the world. As such, IEM is not just a branch of enrollment management, but it is also something much greater than enrollment management because it is so closely connected to international affairs, intercultural communication, and the global economy. Please refer to *NAFSA's International Education Professional Competencies*™ (http://www.nafsa.org/competencies) for a full listing of competencies related to three main functions of IEM: direct service, management, and strategy and policy.

It is important for administrators to recognize the additional knowledge bases, skill sets, and responsibilities required of effective IEM professionals. Failure to do so may lead to domestic enrollment professionals and international enrollment professionals holding the same position classifications, pay grades, and job requirements when in fact the two positions often reflect very different levels of complexity.

Much like the individual gears of a watch or the unique components of an ecosystem, the various pieces of IEM interact to make up a whole that is larger than the sum of its parts. This is because IEM represents a complex system comprised of internal and external elements that operate in a mutually dependent manner. Using the example of international affairs, it is clear that positive relations between the United States and other countries influence the flow of international students from those nations to the United States, but having international alumni who return to their home countries also promote positive relations between the United States and other nations.

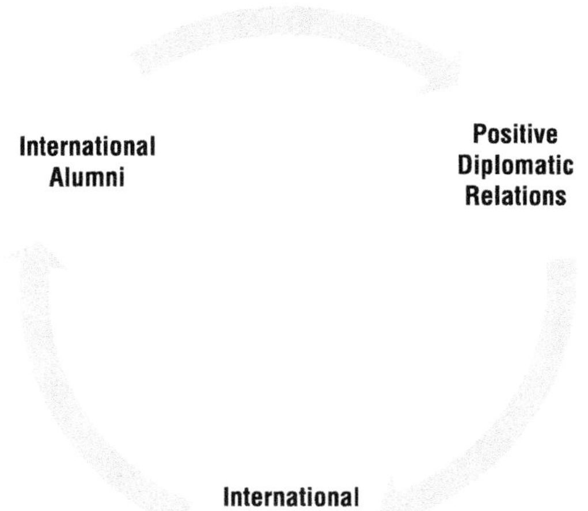

International Alumni

Positive Diplomatic Relations

International Student Enrollment

The IEM system is comprised of several primary subsystems, including international recruitment, admissions, and student services. Each of these may further be broken down into secondary subsystems as indicated by Figure 1.

Figure 1: Subsystems of International Enrollment Management

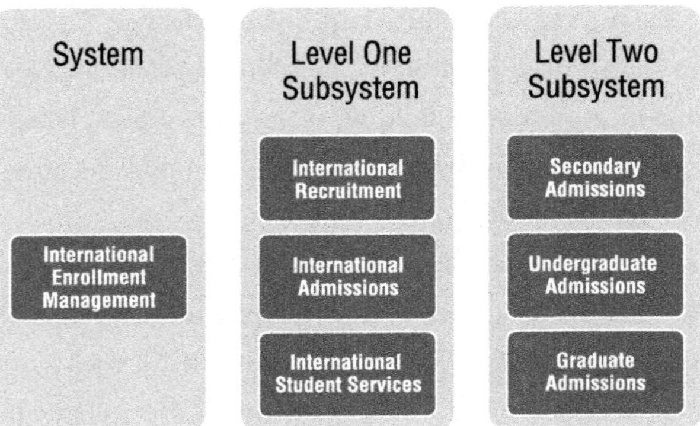

A note on terminology:

After admitting a student to a full course of study, a school's Designated School Official (DSO) must access the Student and Exchange Visitor Information System (SEVIS) to create a SEVIS record for the student and issue a Certificate of Eligibility, which the student then uses to obtain an F-1 visa, to acquire or extend F-1 nonimmigrant status, or to request certain F-1 student benefits. U.S. Department of Homeland Security (DHS) regulations at 8 CFR 214.3(k) establish the conditions that must be met before a DSO can issue a "certificate of eligibility." For F-1 and M-1 students, the certificate of eligibility is designated as Form I-20. The certificate of eligibility produced in a similar way for J-1 exchange visitor students by an exchange visitor program is designated as Form DS-2019. In this book, we generally use the term Form I-20 or Form DS-2019 to identify this form, unless otherwise noted.

It may seem logical to further break down the IEM system into distinct parts (e.g., international credential evaluation and issuance of Form I-20 or Form DS-2019), but a true understanding of IEM comes only when one focuses not just on the parts and subsystems themselves, but on their visible and invisible interactions. This allows one to effectively map complex processes (e.g., international admissions) and see the sum product of essential and nonessential steps, decisions, handoffs, loopbacks, and delays within the international admissions workflow, which otherwise go unnoticed. The relationships that each of these elements have to one another have an incredibly strong impact on an institution's ability to recruit, admit, enroll, and graduate international students.

Summary of Chapters

In this book, experienced international enrollment management professionals representing a wide range of professional backgrounds and organizations volunteered to share their perspectives and experiences related to international admissions. Each chapter is rich in its treatment of an assigned topic; collectively they represent one of the most comprehensive publications currently available on the topic of international admissions.

Chapter 2 addresses the importance of developing a campuswide definition of international students since this is critical not only for clear division of labor, but also for accurate data collection, analysis, and reporting. The author presents key criteria to consider related to this definition and describes various types of international applicants. This chapter is a useful addition to any training materials provided to new international admissions professionals, and it also serves as a valued resource for senior administrators interested in raising awareness of the populations served by international admissions.

Chapter 3 focuses on international admissions issues relevant to public and private secondary schools. The author presents international secondary student enrollment trends, discusses immigration considerations, describes common components of an international application, and outlines special policy considerations for enrolling international students at secondary schools.

In Chapter 4, the author deconstructs the international undergraduate admissions process. Considerations pertaining to issues associated with standardized examinations, proof of English language proficiency, transferring in credit from other institutions, and common internal policies are all presented.

Moving on to international graduate admission, Chapter 5 provides a third perspective on components of the international application that are common within all levels of education, but the author includes analysis of additional issues unique to graduate school admission. She concludes her chapter with advice for working effectively with faculty, improving the quality of communications with applicants, as well as ensuring international graduate students are prepared for success after the admissions process is completed.

Chapter 6 serves as a concise overview of essential considerations and baseline practices related to the evaluation of foreign academic credentials. This chapter is comprehensive enough to be of value to even the most experienced international credential evaluator, but it is also written in a manner that makes this highly technical topic accessible to all.

In Chapter 7, the author examines the seven components of an effective admissions office. While this chapter is written with the director or manager of international admissions in mind, the framework presented has much wider applications for admissions in general. The author's analysis of advantages and disadvantages associated with four distinct office structures will surely be of interest to senior administrators tasked with examining how the international admissions process fits into existing administrative structures.

Chapter 8 is divided into seven parts, each focused on a special topic. Not all of these topics will apply to all institutions, but the knowledge contained in these contributions is applicable to all professionals who wish to more fully understand international admissions as a professional domain. The special topics include:

A. Bridge and Pathway Programs
B. Agents
C. Overseas Representative Offices
D. International Admissions: Financing Higher Education
E. The Nuts and Bolts of International Admissions Operations
F. International-Friendly Application Process
G. Intensive English Programs

Rounding out the publication is Chapter 9, which is a survey of selected resources that are available to international admissions professionals. These range from workshops and conferences to print and online publications.

Conclusion

This publication represents a first attempt by NAFSA's IEM community to compile in-depth knowledge about a broad range of topics pertinent to international admissions in book format. The chapters were written by a diverse group of international admissions professionals who each brought unique knowledge and experiences to this project. While most of the chapters focus on core issues in international admissions, others highlight emerging issues that have received sparse attention to date in both the academic and professional literature. Therefore, this book serves a dual purpose of mapping the current landscape of international admissions while at the same time expanding that landscape by focusing on new and emerging concerns. It also adds to the IEM professional literature by serving as a companion text to *NAFSA's Guide to International Student Recruitment, Third edition* (2017), which is edited by Jessica Black Sandberg of Temple University.

David L. Di Maria

2 International Students

By Lin Larson

There has always been an organic system in place to offer admission to international students to an educational institution. Admissions offices evaluate and review application files, following the protocols established at their campuses. During the time of dramatic growth of applicants from outside the United States, systems and processes needed to be revamped to meet this challenge. We learned of options and best practices from each other. One task that is critical to the success of admitting international students to U.S. institutions is understanding and agreeing upon the definitions or descriptions we collectively use in our work. This chapter focuses on definitions and identifiers related to international students. Sources include a variety of organizations and documents, information from international education colleagues, and knowledge drawn from experience and best practices.

Definitions and Descriptors—Making Sure We Know Who We Are Talking About

International Students

We must clearly define the term "international student." Each institution must also determine how to count and report on students who do not hold a U.S. passport or legal permanent residence (i.e., Green Card), as well as how to account for third culture kids, U.S. passport holders studying outside the United States, refugees, and undocumented students. How does your institution count these distinct groups?

There are many definitions of "international student" and these may vary from institution to institution. Which definition your institution uses is dependent on the mission, organization, climate on campus, and how you report student numbers to the campus administration and to U.S. government agencies. Reporting will be made to the National Center for Education Statistics via the Integrated Postsecondary Education Data System (IPEDS). Your institution will also have its own reporting requirements.

According to IPEDS, a nonresident alien or international student is:

> "A person who is not a citizen or national of the United States and who is in this country on a visa or temporary basis and does not have the right to remain indefinitely. Note: Nonresident aliens are to be reported separately in the places provided, rather than in any of the racial/ethnic categories described above."
> (See https://nces.ed.gov/ipeds/Section/definitions/.)

Included on the web site are the "Definitions for New Race and Ethnicity Categories" now used by institutions in their required reporting; this is to what "categories described above" refers.

A commonly used definition for "international student" was created by UNESCO:

> "An international student is defined as an individual who is enrolled for credit at an accredited higher education institution in the U.S. on a temporary visa, and who is not an immigrant (permanent resident with an I-551 or Green Card), or an undocumented immigrant, or a refugee."

According to the UNESCO Institute for Statistics' (UIS) Global Education Digest (2006), an internationally mobile student has left his or her country, or territory of origin, and moved to another country or territory with the singular objective of studying. This definition is supported by the Organisation for Economic Co-operation and Development's (OECD) Education at a Glance (2016), which makes an important distinction between "international students" and "foreign students" in defining terms for the cross-border-mobility section of its comparative dataset.

Using these definitions, we can surmise that an international student is defined as a "nonimmigrant" visitor who comes to the United States temporarily to take classes, either for a short term of study or for university matriculation. A nonimmigrant student is someone who:

- intends to stay in the United States temporarily;
- does not have U.S. citizenship or legal permanent resident status (a "Green Card");
- applies for a visa to be allowed entry into the United States; and
- has an F-1, J-1, or M-1 student visa (most international students hold one of these statuses).

There are many types of visas beyond the F, J, and M student visas, but these are the most commonly issued visa types when students apply for their study visa. For a complete list of visa types, please see https://travel.state.gov/content/visas/en/general/all-visa-categories.html.

Students must abide by a number of regulations in order to comply with the terms of their immigration status. For instance, undergraduate students must generally be enrolled full time. It is critically important to make sure your Student Information System correctly codes international students so that staff in the International Student Services Office, the Financial Aid Office, the Office of the Registrar, and other key units can appropriately classify international students and their unique needs. Advisers need to be aware of the minimum hours/units enrollment requirements so that they can provide correct academic advice. The Financial Aid Office may need to keep track of state awards, federal funding, and other scholarship offers. The registrar may need to track major requirement completion and degree progress. The International Student Services Office must report key data and events (e.g., enrollment status, address changes, and employment authorization) to the Department of Homeland Security's Student and Exchange Visitor Program (SEVP).

While it seems simple, correct reporting on student status can be challenging. Problems may arise at the time of application if students do not indicate their visa type correctly. There may be institutional differences in ways students are reported. It is critical to work with data stewards to create standards and cross-checks to ensure all students on a visa are correctly coded. Campus constituents should be aware of how to distinguish domestic students from international students using the Student Information System.

Many institutions attempt to proactively resolve potential issues, beginning with the application. Asking the correct questions in logical order will help minimize future confusion. The basic considerations below are useful for thinking through the type of information that may be obtained via questions integrated into the application.

1. Is the applicant a U.S. citizen?
2. If no, then what is the citizenship the applicant used or intends to use to enter the United States?
    a. Note that some applicants may hold more than one citizenship.
3. Does the applicant currently hold a legal immigration status in the United States?
4. If no, then what immigration status does the applicant intend to obtain upon entering the United States?

Students who are Deferred Action Childhood Arrivals (DACA), undocumented, AB540 in California, permanent residents, and Temporary Protected Status (TPS) may or may not be considered international students for reporting purposes. In some cases, they may qualify for in-state tuition at public institutions and other unique benefits.

Types of International Applicants

SECONDARY SCHOOL

You will find detailed information on this category of students in chapter 3. In general, an international high school student is someone who falls within these categories:

- Is enrolled for all years of secondary school, but not a citizen or permanent resident of the United States. Think of a Korean student who is enrolled in school and lives in the United States due to a parent's work assignment, or is living with relatives or others, or living alone for the purpose of study at a U.S. school. Graduation from the U.S. school is likely.
- Is enrolled for part of his/her secondary education, but not a citizen or permanent resident. Think of a student from Germany who enrolled in a local German school for 1–3 years of secondary education, then moves to the United States to graduate with a U.S. diploma. These students have "mixed academic records." Graduation from the U.S. school is probable.
- Is enrolled for a short period of time in a secondary school not within his/her home country. Consider programs like AFS, Youth for Understanding, Rotary Exchange, etc. Graduation from a U.S. school is unlikely.

COLLEGE/UNIVERSITY: NEW FRESHMEN OR FIRST-YEAR STUDENTS

A new freshman has not typically completed any college- or university-level coursework or degree following graduation from secondary school. This student enters a college or university with the intention of matriculating, pursuing an associate's, bachelor's, or first degree (bachelor's degree). There may be exceptions where a recent secondary school student has the option to complete tertiary-level courses following graduation with the permission of the admitting institution. This option might include community college, summer bridge programs, or college preparatory courses. In some cases, a new freshman could enroll with many college credits if he or she completed that work prior to secondary school graduation or is enrolled in a middle college type curriculum.

New international freshman students matriculate from their secondary school and are prepared to enter university. Depending on your institutional organization and regulations, students may be required to be admissible to a similar institution in their home country to be eligible for admission. In other cases, if the student has an adequate academic background that aligns with your admission requirements, he/she can be considered for admission without being eligible for a similar institution in his/her home country.

Admission requirements for international students should mirror those of domestic students. This means testing requirements for the SAT 1 and 2 or ACT, AP, or IB courses should be the same. An additional requirement for a TOEFL, IELTS, or online interview may also be required if the student's language of instruction in secondary school is not English.

TRANSFER STUDENTS

A transfer student is typically defined as one who has completed college- or university-level courses at another postsecondary institution. The student can transfer to another school where those earned credits are accepted in the student's study/graduation plan. In California, for example, community colleges and state universities have agreed on courses that transfer from any in-state community college to a state university. It is in a database accessible to all students who intend to transfer and to any transfer adviser. For more information on California's official repository of articulation, see the Articulation System for Stimulating Interinstitutional Student Transfer at ASSIST.org.

There may be times when transfer credits awarded are a mixture of non-U.S.-based recognized institutions and U.S.-based schools. Consideration of likely equivalencies without a course duplication can be tricky at times. Knowing that your international admissions officer or credential evaluator has been trained in these "mixed records" is an important part of the process.

GRADUATE STUDENTS

A graduate student has completed a first degree (bachelor degree) at an accredited or recognized institution of higher education. In the United States, this first degree is normally a 4-year course of study or equivalent. Graduate degrees include master of arts, master of science, PhD, EdD, LLM, JD, MBA, etc. The area of study to be pursued in a graduate degree does not necessarily have to be in the same area of study as the first degree for studies in social studies, law, business, humanities, and the like. It is highly recommended that students who wish to pursue studies in a Science, Technology, Engineering, and Math (STEM) subject have a strong background in those areas. For example, it is quite difficult to hold a BA in economics and be accepted to a postgraduate course of study in chemical engineering, unless separately qualified due to participation in enrichment programs.

Applicants from universities outside the United States who wish to apply to a graduate program must meet the subject area requirements for admission as any student who may have studied in the United States. Many assessments including the GRE, GMAT, TOEFL, or IELTS may be required of students to qualify for admission consideration. Since there are many configurations for graduate school admission processes, students need to research academic departments to find the one that best suits them, making sure that there are faculty who have similar interests in research, projects, and study emphasis as the student. It is not helpful if the student wishes to pursue research in topic B when the department they wish to apply to only wants students with interests in topic W.

PROFESSIONAL DEGREE

There are about 40 graduate degrees deemed "professional degrees." These are programs in advanced studies to prepare a student in a vocational or professional field. These programs of study can include theoretical materials, but in the end, they must provide knowledge for practical application of the area of study. Master's programs that fall under this category are mostly terminal in scope, not intended for further studies; think MBA, LLM, M.Arch, etc. PhD programs in this category also prepare students for practical application, but may also include training to supervise or teach others, or conduct research to discover new knowledge.

For a list of professional degrees conferred in the United States, please see a list provided by College Confidential at http://talk.collegeconfidential.com/graduate-school/389660-professional-degree-vs-academic-graduate-degree.html.

When considering an international student for admission, research is recommended into the student's academic background, grades or marks, test scores, and all other available information, to the best of the admission officer's ability. Applications should mirror those received from domestic students.

NONDEGREE PROGRAMS

Nondegree programs are available to international students. These programs include, but are not limited to, short-term courses for directed study, certificate courses for professional or interest development, summer school, intensive English programs, or study abroad exchange. Students in nondegree programs do not intend to matriculate or graduate from the institution in which they are enrolled. They are working toward continuing education, language study, or study abroad exchange experiences through an exchange partner or independent provider. Students in such programs may work directly with the school's Office of the Registrar, Summer School Office, Education Abroad Office or Extension Office. Nondegree program admission processes rarely involve the Admissions Office.

SPONSORED STUDENTS

Sponsored students are those for whom expenses such as tuition, fees, and insurance (and sometimes housing and other expenses) are paid directly to the institution by a third party. Funding organizations can include governments, international organizations, nonprofit organizations, foundations, an employer in the home country, or other third-party organization or institution. Funds are not given to the student to pay campus fees. Likewise, study abroad, self-pay, or short-term program students are not considered sponsored students. A few of the better-known funding/sponsor organizations include Saudi Arabia Cultural Mission, Kuwait Cultural Office, The Royal Thai Embassy, Qatar Ministry of Higher Education, Petronas, Majlis Amanah Raykat (MARA), BECAS Chile, and Deutscher Akademischer Austauschdienst (DAAD). Students meet specific requirements established by the organizations for funding and apply directly to these entities.

Sponsored students need to abide by university policy allowing the funding organization access to information regarding tuition and fees, financial aid, and enrollment. Students must also understand their responsibilities to maintain their scholarship funding. Some of these responsibilities include providing the sponsoring agency transcripts, class enrollments, grades, paying balances due not covered by their funding, and clearing any financial blocks that affect receiving grades, transcripts, or a diploma.

Institutions often have an office or specific personnel to work with sponsored students as coordination of funding and payment deadlines can be confusing or difficult.

UNDOCUMENTED STUDENTS

Students who enter the United States without inspection, or overstay their visa term, whether or not they are with their families, are undocumented students. In California, these students can be reported as nonresident aliens or resident aliens. To be a resident alien in California, a student must have a minimum three full academic years of secondary school in the state and must graduate from that school. Such students may enjoy the benefits of California Assembly Bill 540, which provides for access to some financial aid from state institutions.

Federal law does not prohibit the admission of undocumented students to any U.S. college or university, public or private, nor does it require proof of citizenship. Laws vary by each state and institutions develop policies on the admission of undocumented students adhering to state laws to which they are subject. Some universities bar the admission of undocumented students.

ATHLETES

Collegiate sports are available to international students if they meet the university entrance requirements and qualify for the athletic team. Some athletes are recruited by a coach, while others can "walk on" and join the team. There are three divisions in college/university sports: I, II, and III. Divisional status is determined by the National Collegiate Athletic Association (NCAA). Students who wish to be considered for athletics must register with the NCAA in addition to submitting a university admission application. If a student gains admission to an institution of higher education, this decision has no relationship to being guaranteed a spot on an athletic team or an athletic scholarship. In general, athletic team placements and scholarships are made by coaches and other athletic department staff.

Some divisions have the ability to award athletic scholarships to students, while others do not. In most cases, Division I schools have limited full and partial scholarships for students. Some Division II and III schools may have a few scholarships available, depending on the sport the student wishes to play.

For information on registering with the NCAA, please see http://www.ncaa.org.

ONLINE COURSES

Online courses have become very popular and easier to access over the past five years. Many courses are rigorous enough to fulfill university-level graduation or major area of study requirements and be transferred to a university where the student attends courses in person. Some online courses provide complete programs in academic areas of study that culminate in a degree. Other courses may be taken for foundation work or simply for interest.

Massive Open Online Courses (MOOCs) are offered by universities to enable students to pursue subjects of interest. These courses rarely qualify for college/university credit.

It can be confusing when investigating online courses, so here are basic descriptions of different types of online courses:

- Online schools are credit-granting institutions that offer the majority of their courses through Internet-based methods.

- Online course publishers develop curriculum and sell or license their courses for delivery by an institution.
- Online courses offered by an institution for credit are reflected in the institution's course catalog and mirror in-person courses.

Attending class via the Internet does not require students to move from their current homes. No visas for study are required. Admissions processes can differ from institution to institution depending upon the type of course in which the student wishes to enroll. When investigating an online program or course, it is important to consider the accreditation or recognition of the institution offering the courses; without such recognition, courses cannot transfer to a regionally accredited U.S. university.

YOUNGER STUDENTS

When we talk about younger or "underage" students, we refer to students who have not yet reached their 18th birthdays when they enroll at a college or university. There will be students who become 18 during the first few months of enrollment, and these students are not the population we are discussing. We are discussing students between the ages of 12 and 17. While uncommon, there are students in that age range who can and have been admitted to institutions of higher education.

There is no set policy for these students. There are safety, liability, and health concerns for these younger students. Colleges and universities may have restrictions when it comes to on-campus housing. Since these students are under 18, a responsible adult may need to sign housing contracts and required medical authorization forms, as needed.

When underage U.S. students enter a university, they might remain at home and remain a responsibility of the parents. By comparison, for international students, living with parents or another guardian may not be possible. Options might include living with a relative or vetted host family. Some student families may have the resources to purchase a home, or provide an older sibling or even a nanny to accompany the student. Recently, it has become "normal" for a young student to live alone while attending school. A number of freshman applicant Personal Statements attest to the difficulty of being alone and responsible for homework, cooking, cleaning, and paying bills.

Considering the relative maturity levels of underage students, institutions may wish to consider admission on a case-by-case basis.

Secondary school-age students face many of the same issues as university students. Procedures and guidelines should only be established after careful consideration of the type of school—boarding or day school, public or private—into which the student is enrolling. Issues of housing, health care decisions, and adjustment to life without family at a young age can be challenging.

Conclusion

Now that we understand who is considered an international student and some of the special considerations, restrictions, and situations that affect their enrollment at an institution of higher education in the United States, take a moment to assess your institution. Are you following "best practices" in reporting and working with this population? Do changes need to be implemented? Depending on the size of your campus, changes in procedures can be easy to implement or difficult to explain. The key to a strong international admissions program is a thorough understanding of the international population being served and consistency in administering policies.

3 International Admissions at Secondary Schools

By Amy VanSurksum

Secondary schools are defined by the U.S. Department of State as "including grades 9-12" (U.S. Department of State 2016). International students have been studying at secondary schools in the United States for nearly a century. Secondary-level student exchanges were introduced by Rotary Clubs in Europe as early as the 1920s. Since that time, student numbers have increased significantly. Secondary students can study in the United States as exchange or fee-paying students. They can study at public and private secondary schools. They can live with host families or attend boarding schools. Some study for a short period of time to learn English or have an international experience. Others study for full high school diplomas with the intent to continue their education at U.S. postsecondary institutions or return home. No matter the intent or duration of study, secondary-level international students will likely continue to be a growing population.

Numbers of International Students in U.S. Secondary Schools

The most recent publication on international secondary students in the United States produced by the Institute of International Education (IIE) in 2014 reported 73,019 international secondary students studied in the United States in 2013. Of that number, 67 percent came on F-1 student visas and 33 percent came on J-1 exchange student visas (IIE 2014). International students at the secondary level come from a different mix of countries of origin compared with those studying at higher education institutions in the United States. IIE reported the top 10 countries of origin for international secondary students in 2013 (see http://www.iie.org/Research-and-Publications/Publications-and-Reports/IIE-Bookstore/Charting-New-Pathways-To-Higher-Education-International-Secondary-Students-In-The-United-States#.WLboPWU1ZFI).

Only 1 percent of U.S. secondary school students are international students. The majority of degree-seeking international students come from Asian countries, including China, South Korea, Vietnam, Japan, Thailand, Taiwan, and Hong Kong. Visiting students from Latin America and Europe typically study short-term for a cultural experience or language immersion for one year or less.

Public Versus Private Secondary Schools

Public secondary schools or districts can apply for approval from the U.S. Department of Homeland Security's Student and Exchange Visitor Program (SEVP) to issue Form I-20s to international students, which allow the students to apply for F-1 student visas. Students must be enrolled full time, but are limited to 12 months of study. F-1 students must pay the full unsubsidized cost to attend a public secondary school. Public schools or districts can also accept J-1 exchange students from organizations approved by the Department of State. J-1 exchange students must be enrolled full time, and can come for one semester or one year.

Private or independent schools can also apply for approval to issue Form I-20s. Students must enroll full time and may stay for a program's full duration in order to earn a high school diploma. Private or independent schools may also accept J-1 exchange students.

Admission Considerations

Secondary school applications for admission of F-1 international students should follow the same conditions as other education levels in order to be eligible for issuance of Form I-20s. According to 8 CFR 214.3(k):

1. The prospective student has made a written application to the school.
2. The written application, the student's transcripts or other records of courses taken, proof of financial responsibility for the student,

and other supporting documents have been received, reviewed, and evaluated at the school's location in the United States.

3. The appropriate school authority has determined that the prospective student's qualifications meet all standards for admission.
4. The official responsible for admission at the school has accepted the prospective student for enrollment in a full course of study.

Specific guidance for enrolling J-1 exchange students at the secondary level should be carefully reviewed and can be found at 22 CFR 62.25.

Required Components of the Application

- Application Form: The application form can be completed by the applicant, parent, or legal guardian (for F-1 students), or a designated sponsoring organization (for J-1 exchange students).
  - In addition to collecting the applicant's general demographics, educational history, and contact information on the application form, collecting detailed contact information for both parents and/or any legal guardians is critically important when working with students under the age of 18. If someone other than a legal guardian or parent will be given guardianship rights while the student resides in the United States, then written documentation should be obtained. On occasion, families will identify a spokesperson who will act as an intermediary between the school and the family, but who is not a legal guardian. It is important for each individual school to consider how such arrangements will be handled.
- Academic Records: It is model practice to request that official academic records be sent directly to the receiving school by the issuing school or organization, especially if classes completed at another school will be evaluated for credit toward a high school diploma. Primary- or middle-school-level credentials are typically as accessible as secondary school credentials. Refer to the same model practices and

considerations for obtaining educational credentials as recommended for postsecondary academic records. Literal English translations should be requested when credentials are issued in a language other than English.

- Financial Certification: Applicants are required to provide proof of available funds to cover the full cost of tuition, school fees, room, and board. The estimated costs associated with attending secondary school, including living expenses, should be reviewed on an annual basis.
  - Public schools issuing Form I-20s must receive reimbursement for tuition and fees upon admission. The F-1 visa will not be issued without proof of payment noted on the Form I-20 or an accompanying notarized statement from the Designated School Official (DSO).
  - While medical insurance is not currently mandated by immigration regulations for F-1 students, it is highly recommended. Consular officers have the discretion to ask for proof that visa applicants can afford medical expenses while studying in the United States. J-1 exchange students are required to carry medical insurance that meets or exceeds the minimum coverage requirements specified at 22 CFR 62.14 for the duration of their stay the United States.

Optional Components of the Application

- Standardized Testing and Language Proficiency: Depending on the level of English language support offered at a secondary school, an applicant's English proficiency may be evaluated as part of the application process. While many secondary school applicants take the TOEFL or IELTS, these exams are not designed for the developmental level of younger language learners. Standardized exams appropriate for the age and grade level of the applicant should be encouraged, when possible. The following list is in no way exhaustive, but provides a few examples of level-appropriate standardized tests for secondary-level admission consideration:

- TOEFL Junior—English proficiency exam
- SSAT—assessment test used by some independent schools to measure basic verbal, math, and reading skills
- International Baccalaureate (IB) Middle Years Programme (MYP): assessment leads to course results and MYP certificate (typically taken at age 16 or upon completion of Middle Years Programme).

- Developmental, Behavioral, and Emotional Evaluations: Unlike the U.S. secondary educational system, many countries do not have a formal process to assess and support students with developmental, behavioral, or emotional disabilities or challenges. In the United States, a student who has a documented Individualized Educational Plan (IEP) or 504 Plan can take his or her documentation to a new school to request support. Special needs are not always disclosed or identified during the application process for international students. Anticipation by the receiving school that special needs may exist among its international student population can initiate proactive staffing and policy development for supporting diverse needs.
- Letters of Recommendation: Letters of recommendation can provide added insight into a student's application. If specific information is desired to better support or evaluate incoming students, consider providing a template with required questions for the recommender. For example, an academic recommendation letter can help with course placement, while a principal or counselor recommendation can disclose special needs and behavioral patterns.
- Interviews: Interviewing is a useful screening tool in the secondary admissions process. It is common for a parent or agent to complete the application form on behalf of the applicant, in which case it is important to determine the language proficiency, maturity, and

academic goals and background of the applicant directly. In-person interviews or interviews utilizing video-conferencing technology provide the most transparent experience.

Special Considerations for Secondary Students

- Determining Placement: International students should be placed in a grade level that most closely matches the level at which they would be studying in their home country. Repeating years—or holding a student back—and grade skipping should only be considered in situations that would normally be recommended for a domestic student. Placement testing can be used to determine the most accurate placement for each individual student. Consideration should be given to the sequence in which subjects are taught in the home country. For example, if physics is normally offered in grade 9 at the U.S. school, but in grade 11 in the home country, place the student according to the subjects they have not yet had the opportunity to study. Flexible class scheduling can benefit the student regardless of his or her desired outcome—returning to the home country secondary system or applying to U.S. postsecondary institutions upon completion of high school.
- Parents and Guardians: Parents and guardians play a critical role in the success and support of secondary-level students. Parents or guardians of international students may live far away. In some cases, language and cultural barriers may also exist. Issues such as access to student information, academic performance, disciplinary actions, permission to participate in activities and trips, and medical situations are a few situations that warrant proactive consideration on the part of the receiving school. Legal liabilities, on-site guardianship, and releases of information should be carefully explored before welcoming international students to the school.
- Homestay Issues: If a school plans to house international students with local host families, it is important to be familiar with the specific

requirements listed at 22 CFR 62.25. Additionally, the sponsor should consider other legal and ethical issues that can arise as a result of placing secondary students in homestays.

Conclusion

As international students increasingly look to the United States for secondary education, school administrators have a responsibility to consider the best interests of the students they invite into their community. Meeting this responsibility requires close collaboration between teachers, school counselors, school administrators and community hosts. By clearly defining admission requirements and processes, understanding immigration regulations that apply to the international students they attract, and establishing risk management practices and policies, both secondary-level students and schools will be set up for success.

References

Institute of International Education (IIE). 2014. "Charting New Pathways to Higher Education: International Secondary Students in the United States." New York: Institute of International Education.

NAFSA Adviser's Manual 360. NAFSA: Association of International Educators. Annual subscription to content of online publication. www.nafsa.org/themanual.

Page, Andrew. 2013. *The History of Rotary Youth Exchange*. Presentation at the 2013 Youth Exchange Officers Preconvention Meeting, Lisbon, Portugal, July 8, 2013. Retrieved from http://www.slideshare.net/Rotary_International/history-of-rotary-youth-exchange.

U.S. Department of State. "Foreign Students in Public Schools." Accessed September 30, 2016. https://travel.state.gov/content/visas/en/study-exchange/student/foreign-students-in-public-schools.html.

4 International Undergraduate Admissions Issues

By Mandy Hansen

International undergraduate admissions is a process that requires staff with the ability to mesh current review processes for domestic applicants with the nuanced aspects of international applicants. Experience with intercultural communication along with expertise in foreign credential analysis, data analysis, and immigration regulations is required. Applicants from non-Native English-speaking countries may find the application process confusing. A trained admissions professional is able to communicate in simple and easy-to-understand terms across cultures; such communication is required in a timely manner and reliable e-mail is essential to an operation's success. Considerations in the international admissions process include standardized exams, English language proficiency, essays, transcripts, transfer credit, advanced placement, financial support, conditional admission, data management, as well as accommodations for special application materials like auditions.

Standardized Exams

The Scholastic Aptitude Test (SAT) and American College Test (ACT) are two standardized entry exams commonly used during the domestic admissions review. These two tests are offered internationally. Keep in mind, however, that these entry exams may not be offered in every country. Additionally these exams are U.S.-centric as the context of the questions relates to materials taught in a U.S. classroom and may cause problems and lower test scores for students originating from a local secondary school abroad.

Therefore, applicants from local secondary schools abroad may have difficulty with the questions and score low on certain sections of the exams due to differences in the education systems and unfamiliarity with the cultural context of the questions. Recognizing these issues will allow admissions offices to set criteria for admission that is more flexible and possibly to exempt students from these exams or place higher consideration on transcripts and other test scores such as English proficiency exams. In addition, some higher education institutions in the United States may take the SAT or ACT verbal score in lieu of an English proficiency exam.

English Language Proficiency

Fluency in English contributes to academic success as reading, writing, and speaking skills are essential for classroom participation, note-taking, written assignments, and group projects. A consideration in the international admissions process is a student's ability to succeed in a U.S. higher education classroom measured via English proficiency. There are a variety of measures to assess a student's English proficiency. Therefore, it is important to have an admissions policy in place in which English proficiency minimum scores are clearly available for applicants. In addition, a policy is recommended for when an English proficiency score will be waived; for example, if a student is originating from a country in which English is the native language of instruction, if the student attended all of her secondary school with English instruction, or if the student is transferring from a higher education institution with significant coursework in English.

It is recommended that experts in such exams be consulted prior to setting minimum scores in addition to connecting with peer institutions or similar institutions on their policies, scores, and tests. Experts include professionals such as intensive English instructors, intensive English program directors, intensive English test administrators, or international admissions professionals.

Below are examples of some common English language proficiency exams. Please note that this is not meant to be an exhaustive list as there are many English proficiency exams that may be considered in addition to home-grown institutional exams that higher education institutions may utilize for placement into English courses for non-native and native English speakers. Comparison charts are widely available on commonly offered English proficiency exams that offer test comparisons that can assist in establishing admissions criterion.

TOEFL: The Test of English as a Foreign Language (TOEFL) is a common English proficiency assessment used by higher education institutions and admissions offices to measure English language ability. It is administered by ETS and is widely available in an Internet version (TOEFL iBT) but may only be offered in certain countries in paper-based format (TOEFL PBT). Components of the TOEFL iBT include an overall score ranging from 0-120 and subscores in reading, speaking, listening, and writing that range from 0-30.

IELTS: The International English Language Testing System (IETLS) is another common English proficiency exam used by higher education institutions around the world. This assessment is jointly owned by the British Council, IDP: IELTS Australia, and Cambridge English Language Assessment. It uses a band of scores ranging from 0–9 and includes subscores and sections in reading, speaking, listening, and writing. The overall band score is an average of each section's subscores.

PTE: The Pearson Test of English Academic (PTE Academic) is another English proficiency exam. The scores range from 10–90 and include overall English score, as well as scores for individual English subskills and enabling skills. The PTE Academic includes an overall score, speaking score, listening score, reading score, writing score, grammar score, spelling score, oral fluency score, vocabulary score, and written discourse score.

MELAB: The Michigan English Language Assessment Battery (MELAB) is a standardized test created via a joint venture between the University of Michigan and the University of Cambridge called CaMLA. The test evaluates proficiency in understanding, writing, and speaking the English language. It includes sections on writing, listening, and grammar/vocabulary/reading comprehension, and includes an optional speaking section. There is a final MELAB score reported ranging from 0–99, and subscores vary based upon the area (for example, writing is 0–97 while the optional speaking section is 1–4).

ITEP: The International Test of English Proficiency (iTEP) is administered by Boston Educational Services and is an Internet-based exam taken at a test center. The iTEP includes sections on listening, reading, writing, grammar, and speaking, with scores ranging from 0–6, and an overall score of 0–6.

College Essays and Letters of Recommendation

Essays and letters of recommendation are used in admissions to gauge the writing skills of the applicant as well garner insight into the applicant. The essay or personal statement is often used in a comprehensive admissions process to learn more about the applicant. Questions utilized for international applicants need to be culturally sensitive, as applicants abroad may have difficulty with composing an open reply or responding to a question that is U.S. centric.

Special considerations for letters of recommendation are needed from applicants originating from local schools abroad as many secondary institutions abroad do not have guidance counselors. A lack of staff with proficiency in English may be a challenge for international student applicants, sometimes resulting in letters of recommendation that are a basic testament to success instead of a well-developed insightful recommendation. In addition, you may see letters of recommendation that appear form-like with similar messaging for different students due to limited English proficiency of the person writing the letter. Therefore, admissions professionals must carefully weigh the value placed on the letter of recommendation in a comprehensive review of international applicants.

Application Fee

The cost of the application fees may vary, with many institutions charging a higher fee than for domestic applicants due to the extra processing and mailing costs. Considerations with setting an appropriate application fee include researching the fees of peer institutions. In addition, a higher application fee may be warranted if it helps to decrease processing and response times and the express mailing of acceptance material to applicants.

To facilitate the payment of an application fee from abroad, it is imperative that the payment system permits international addresses and the use of an international credit card. Alternate payment methods may need to be considered as some international students may be from cash-based economies and will not have access to a credit card. It is important for institutions to accept alternate methods or payment at a later date in addition to offering an option to submit an application for admission without payment. The option for a wire transfer from abroad must be made, and information on this process should be shared (note: a wire transfer fee is often accompanied with bank fees and it is important to establish if the sending or receiving bank is responsible for the wire transfer fees).

Waivers may be considered just as they may with domestic applicants. Some initial questions to address with waivers include: (a) whether the fee will be waived if the student met with an admissions professional, (b) whether the application fee will be waived if the student is originating from a partner school, or (c) whether the fee will be waived to increase applications from international applicants as part of a campaign. It is important to monitor the "admissions funnel" and to gather such data to help tell the story of applications to enrolled students from year to year.

Application Deadlines

Application deadlines vary from institution to institution in the United States. Many institutions maintain the same deadline as the one in place for domestic students, while others have different deadlines to accommodate international students who are seeking admission later in the application process. Factors include reviewing institutional enrollment goals for international applicants and determining if there is a need for deadlines that will allow later international applicants to apply. It is also important to recognize and accommodate spring semester applicants for both freshmen and transfer students.

Transcripts

Grade reports are crucial in the evaluation of international applicants. International admissions staff need to have expertise in foreign credential evaluation, which is an art in converting the local grade system into a U.S. equivalency. Foreign credit evaluation services make it easier for admissions officers without such expertise to understand the degrees, grade systems and credentials. However, there is an extra cost and time commitment for the acquisition of a foreign credit evaluation, which may hinder some international students from applying or selecting your institution as a place to study. Often a course-by-course evaluation will be needed for transfer credit, and credential evaluation services may require an English translation as well as clear legible copies of graduate certificates or diplomas in addition to academic transcripts.

Final Transcripts and Exit Exam Reports

Review for admission during the last year is a factor in domestic admissions (i.e., an admissions decision made with semester 1 grades for the senior year). However, a final transcript may not be available in the same format as it is for a student originating from the United States or an American school-based system. Therefore, an additional consideration in reviewing transcripts is the acceptance of local exit exams in lieu of a grade report. Many institutions of higher education in the United States will accept such reports instead of a student's grade report, as these are acceptable for admission into the student's home country university system. Examples of local exit exams that you may wish to use in lieu of a grade report include the Western African Exam Council (WAEC) in Nigeria or A-levels in UK-based systems.

Official Transcripts and Certified Transcripts

Official transcripts are readily available in the United States and at American-based secondary schools. However, an official transcript from a student originating from other secondary or postsecondary schools may be difficult to acquire. In addition, such a transcript may be individually created upon request by the school and account for some differences in the way that classes show or grades are posted. (For example, the course for Marxism may be written as Marxism 200 or Study of Marxism and be posted on one transcript with a "B" and another with an "86%" even if it is originating from the same school.) Additionally, some countries may only issue one official transcript to a student. Therefore, it is recommended that you accept a certified copy. A certified copy can be obtained from the EducationUSA office (a U.S. Department of State network of more than 400 international student advising centers in more than 170 countries) or be attested via another local source such as the school directly, or other official source.

Translated Transcripts

There are thousands of languages and it is impossible to have admissions staff fluent in every language. Therefore, a policy is needed regarding translated transcripts. An English copy can be submitted that may be the original English translation or a certified copy of the English translation to aid staff in making a decision.

Grading Scales

Grading scales vary within the United States, and such variance occurs abroad within and among countries. Grading scales are provided for evaluation that will equate and make recommendations on grade equivalencies to typical U.S.-based grade scales (i.e., 0–100 or an A–F scale).

Community Colleges

Students entering from community colleges constitute a domestic, "international" market. These international students may already be in the United States or may have completed an associate's degree at an international branch campus or U.S. community college. Many are interested in completing a bachelor's degree after their associate's degree. A policy on transfer pathways and articulation will assist with international students transferring from a community college. These policies may be discussed between a registrar's office, international office, and international admissions or domestic admissions office and can be managed by the international admissions expert on campus.

Facilitation of such agreements often resides with the international admissions office or the international office, and requires close collaboration on such partnerships and the articulation process. In addition, international students may be attending a community college or junior college in their home country. These students will be interested in transfer credit and will want to know the importance of their postsecondary grades in relation to secondary grades in the admissions review process as well as transfer credit.

General Education Development or High School Admission

A General Education Development (GED) diploma is a substitute for a traditional high school or secondary school diploma and is awarded after passing a test. International students may be seeking admission through a country-specific GED program or even from a GED program in the United States that may be offered at a high school or community college. Additionally, international students may be attending high schools in your state. Considerations in admission include the years of enrollment, if any foreign transcripts are needed, and whether the student was in an intensive English track versus fully integrated into degree- or credit-bearing institutional-level classes. Students who are already in the United States may be transferring their immigration status to your school.

Career and Vocational Schools

International applicants may be attending a career or vocational school within or outside the United States. Visiting the policy on admission and transfer credit on the domestic side will aid you in determining admission for international applicants applying with transcripts from such institutions.

Advanced Placement

There exist a variety of ways that an international student can enter into a postsecondary institution with advanced placement. These include but are not limited to the following:

- **International Baccalaureate (IB):** IB programs are expanding around the world. A policy is often in place for domestic applicants that can be shared and applied to international applicants. Oftentimes credit is offered based upon higher level results.
- **Advanced Placement (AP):** These exams are offered domestically as well as in some international locations. A policy can be followed that is implemented for domestic admissions and may offer transfer credit based upon the specific score for the AP exam taken.
- **A-levels:** United Kingdom-based systems offer A-level and AS-level exams. Transfer credit may often be offered for students entering with A-level or AS-level exam scores based upon grade(s) for that specific exam. Students from such systems take a limited number of A-level and AS-level exams and the scores will inform whether transfer credit can be granted.
- **Country Specific:** Scandinavian countries and other countries such as Germany may have secondary school systems in which the student is eligible for transfer credit work based upon the last year of coursework. This last year of work can be considered equivalent to a freshman year of coursework in the United States.

Establishing a policy for credit for any of the above will require research and close collaboration with the office that grants transfer credit and advance placement. Recommendations for moving forward include consulting with a foreign credit evaluation service you value as well as connecting with peer institutions to research policies on advance placement and transfer credit for students.

Personal Résumé, Portfolio, and Auditions

Personal Résumé

If a personal résumé is part of your admissions criterion you may need instructions on how to submit a personal resume. Directed questions will help international applicants to gather information on volunteering, work, and travel that will help you learn about the applicant and determine fit at your institution.

Portfolio and Auditions

International applicants are often unable to visit campus and participate in open houses and in-person activities. It is important to permit portfolios and audition materials to be submitted electronically. For example, an in-person audition for a music program may be impossible for international applicants to participate in due to the distance and expense of international flights. Determining how technology can be used to allow international applicants to fulfill such requirements demonstrate that you are an international friendly campus and can help attract a more diverse student population and talent from afar.

Coding and Tracking of Data

Admissions staff are on the front line and serve as the stewards of initial student data on a college or university campus. It is important to correctly code and track data on international applicants as it relates to both admissions and alumni relations. A specialized approach is needed for international students as the admissions process and associated coding do not fit neatly into a domestic model. Specific modeling and tools are needed to help with international-specific data such as enrollment numbers (degree-seeking, nondegree), retention, coding, and international addresses. Benchmarking is often lacking on the international side while abundant on domestic side (national level). This creates a need for internal data analysis and the ability to pull accurate international student information. Additionally, despite all of the technology that can be used to facilitate admissions decisions and processing, there is still a need for manual review of some materials for international applicants. A human touch is needed on such files due to variety in transcripts, messaging, and issuance of visa documents.

Verification of Financial Support and Visa Documents

A key component to an international student's entry into the United States on a student visa is proof of financial support (such as a bank statement). This proof is required in order for an institution to issue the Form I-20 or Form DS-2019 and for the student's visa interview at the U.S. consulate in her home country. A student needs both an offer of admission and a Form I-20 or Form DS-2019 in order to get her visa. Considerations for international admission include the collection of such documents and whether they should be collected up front with the academic credentials or separately after the offer of admission. International applicants essentially have two parts to their "application" to the school: Part 1, the application for admission to the school, and Part 2, the visa document side of their materials. A major benefit in collecting all materials up front, inclusive of financial support, includes quicker processing and issuance of the Form I-20 or Form DS-2019, which can result in the student getting both the admissions decision and visa document simultaneously in the mail.

Ensure that there is a process in place to review for academic admission without financial support so that the admission of applicants is not halted. Also make sure that admissions staff are able to evaluate and understand financial support documents from around the world, including currency conversion and documents that constitute acceptable financial proof.

Conditional Admission

Conditional admission refers to a student gaining admission to an intensive English program as well as a university-degree-level program. Often these students lack the necessary English skills but meet the academic criteria of the institution (such as grade point average, or GPA). There are governing regulations that restrict the issuance of visa documents to both intensive English and a major or degree program. However, institutions can still consider conditional admission for international applicants. An admissions policy needs to be established for applicants since many international students originate from non-native English-speaking countries and may need intensive English courses before starting their academic-level coursework. Historically, conditional admission options have been important for government-sponsored students whose sponsoring agency requires admission to both an intensive English program and the degree program. It is a consideration for international admissions as such a policy can positively impact international enrollments.

Other Categories of Applicants

There are a variety of application categories that fall outside a typical international student's nonimmigrant status. Examples include Deferred Action for Childhood Arrivals, Refugees, Asylees, American Indians born in Canada, U.S. Territory Applicants and Other Nonimmigrant Applicants.

Deferred Action for Childhood Arrivals (DACA) Applicants

DACA is an immigration policy established in 2012 that allows certain undocumented immigrants to receive a renewable work permit and enjoy the benefit of deferred removal action for a specific period of time, but it does not provide lawful status. These students often have significant schooling in the United States. It is important for state institutions to understand their tuition policy for such applicants and for a process of admission to be set up on the domestic side that allows such students to apply and enroll (regardless of being a private or public institution of higher education).

Refugee and Asylee Applicants

The United States has a history of welcoming refugees and asylees. These individuals are given a pathway to permanent residency and are immigrants to the United States (versus an F-1 international student that is a nonimmigrant as she is only in the United States to study and then is expected to return home after the completion of such studies). Admissions staff need to establish a protocol on who (international or domestic admissions) will review such applicants and if they should apply via an international or domestic application for admission. A process that is flexible and accommodating for such applicants is advised as such applicants may have schooling abroad as well as difficulty in obtaining such credentials due to wars, persecution, or natural disasters.

American Indians Born in Canada

American Indians born in Canada cannot typically be denied entry to the United States. These individuals are also entitled to permanent residence, if they declare intent to permanently reside in the United States. Applicants who fall within this category will likely apply as Canadian citizens, but may be classified as permanent residents by the time they report to the campus.

Applicants from U.S. Territories

Applicants from certain U.S. territories, such as Guam and Puerto Rico, are considered U.S. citizens at birth. However, applicants from other U.S. territories, such as American Samoa and Swains Island, are usually considered U.S. nationals, but not citizens.

Other Nonimmigrant Visa Types

There are a variety of other nonimmigrant visa types that extend beyond the F-1 and J-1 nonimmigrant student visas. Many of these have specific immigration rules regarding enrollment and it is advised that such applicants work closely with international admissions and international student services office to determine admissibility and visa compliance. Training and resources are needed to appropriately advise such applicants and to help such an applicant maintain his or her nonimmigrant status. Some typical nonimmigrant visas seen in an international admissions process aside from F and J applicants include applicants on an A-1, H-1B, or H-4 visa. Unless the student wishes to change status to F-1 or J-1, proof of financial support is not required as issuance of a Form I-20 or Form DS-2019 is not required.

Connecting With International Student and Scholar Services

In order to issue visa documents, institutions must comply with mandatory SEVIS reporting specific to the F-1 and J-1 categories. If this is not done correctly, an institution is at risk of losing its ability to issue visa documents for international students as well as the ability to host and enroll international students on their campus. Admissions offices and the international student and scholar services office must partner closely to ensure immigration compliance and international student success, as well as a smooth transition from the admissions process to arrival on campus. An international office or international student and scholar services division can include English as a Second

Language (ESL) support, tutoring, mentoring, and club and student activities, and often serves as an international education resource to the campus and local community.

Conclusion

In sum, there are a variety of components and issues that institutions must consider in international undergraduate admissions. Knowledge and expertise are required in the areas of intercultural communication and educational systems around the world. The breadth of knowledge required for international admissions may seem daunting, but this book is an excellent resource as are the following professional organizations: NAFSA: Association for International Educators (NAFSA), World Education Services (WES), American International Recruitment Council (AIRC), National Association for College Admission Counseling (NACAC), and the American Association of Collegiate Registrars and Admissions Officers (AACRAO).

5 Graduate Admissions Issues

By Ujjaini Sahasrabudhe

Enrollment trends as revealed through the Institute of International Education (IIE)'s *Open Doors* report indicate that the number of international students attending U.S. institutions continues to grow exponentially each year. According to the 2016 report, nearly 37 percent of all international students enrolled at U.S. colleges and universities were pursuing graduate-level degrees (Institute of International Education 2016). Based on the 350 institutions that responded to its annual survey, the Council of Graduate Schools reported that U.S. universities received more than 1.6 million applications for graduate programs for fall 2015. International applications made up nearly one-half of all graduate applications at these institutions (Council of Graduate Schools 2015). Given this data, and the fact that international students represent a growing percentage of overall graduate enrollments in the United States, the importance of developing a better understanding of international graduate admissions cannot be underestimated.

Whether or not an institution follows a centralized or decentralized graduate admissions model determines the overall operation and enrollment management strategy. However, the basic admissions requirements for international students seeking to pursue graduate degrees in the United States remain more or less the same across institutions.

Admissions Requirements

English Language Proficiency

The ability to communicate effectively in English—to read, write, and speak the language fluently—is vital to success as a graduate student at U.S. universities. Nearly all universities therefore require that prospective students demonstrate their proficiency in English as part of the application process.

Most services that provide English language testing have tests that are designed to measure language skills holistically. Results are reported on numeric scales across areas such as listening, speaking, hearing, and writing as well as an overall performance score.

Common objective measurements of English language proficiency are the Test of English as a Foreign Language (TOEFL), which is administered by ETS, the International English Language Testing System (IELTS), jointly administered by the British Council, IDP: IELTS Australia, and the Cambridge English Language Assessment, and the Pearson Test of English (PTE), administered by Pearson.

Once an institution has determined which test(s) it is going to accept, it is important to use its academic standards to set minimum acceptable scores. Institutions may set a universal minimum that applies across all graduate programs, or minimums may be set at a programmatic or school level. Institutions must also decide whether their minimum standards are for admission or placement purposes. Admissions minimums mean that students who score below set standards will not be eligible for admission at that institution. On the other hand, setting a base score for placement purposes would allow institutions to admit qualified students conditionally as long as they take additional tests and/or English as a Second Language (ESL) classes prior to or alongside their graduate programs. Please refer to the section on bridge and pathway programs in chapter 8 to learn more about conditional admission based on language proficiency levels.

Finally, institutions must determine when international students can be exempt from the English language proficiency-testing requirement. Whether it is waiving the requirement based on earning a bachelor's degree in the United States, being a native of a country whether English is an official language, or earning a degree at an institution where the medium of instruction is English, it is important that an institution is transparent about its standards so that international students have a clear understanding of what is expected of them when they apply.

Standardized Tests

In addition to English proficiency requirements, institutions may also require prospective international students to submit additional test scores such as the GRE, GRE Subject, or GMAT. Minimum acceptable standards for these test scores are usually set at a programmatic level and are applicable to all prospective students.

There are some considerations to keep in mind when setting standardized tests as an admission requirement for international students. Students from certain countries or regions of the world may have limited access to testing facilities or may have trouble signing up for these tests due to how infrequently they are offered. In such circumstances, institutions may consider providing academically strong students alternative tests, specific to the institution perhaps, or offering conditional admission so that students have additional time to take these tests and submit results.

Finally, it is important to keep in mind that standardized tests and the testing environment in general may be contextually unfamiliar for some international students. As a result, their performance on the tests may not be an accurate representation of their academic ability, thus reiterating the need for a more holistic approach to graduate admission, especially when considering prospective international students.

Transcripts

Other countries may use terminology such as statement of results, notification of results, or mark sheets to refer to transcripts. It is therefore useful to describe transcripts more generically when providing international admission requirements, perhaps as academic records or academic performance results, so that it can be more universally understood.

Since many international institutions only provide students with official transcripts in the original language of instruction, English translations must be listed as part of the international admission requirement. It is important for institutions to make it clear to students that personal translations will not be acceptable, and that they must seek the services of professional translation agencies. It is best practice for institutions to require both the original language transcript as well as a professional English translation, and not rely on the translated document exclusively. While translations are meaningful in reviewing coursework, institutions should review format, layout, and, if possible, grades from the original language transcript in order to ensure accuracy. Some U.S. institutions may contract with specific translation services to maintain quality and standardization, a practice that is useful when international students seek guidance on translating their original language transcripts.

Institutions must walk the tightrope between considering cultural context and ensuring qualitative standards when setting transcript requirements for international students. Depending on the country of study, requirements could range from paying a substantial fee in order to obtain official transcripts, completing a military assignment, being present in person to obtain records, or being provided only one copy of the official academic record. Foreign institutions may also refuse to mail official transcripts directly to U.S. universities due to budgetary and manpower issues. At the same time, U.S. institutions must guard themselves against inauthentic academic records and should therefore uphold certain standards as far as transcript submission is concerned.

Giving international students an option to upload or mail in a copy of their university-issued transcript for initial review purposes may save them considerable money and effort. Once a student is being considered for final review or is determined to be admissible, U.S. universities could request official transcripts directly from the student's institution. Alternately, international students could be conditionally admitted and be required to send their final, official transcript to the institution within a stipulated time period (usually before the end of their first semester).

It is important to have trained international credential evaluators on the graduate admission team to determine degree equivalencies and to review academic records for authenticity. Evaluators should also have the ability to be flexible within reason in order to accommodate unusual circumstances when a student is unable to provide official transcripts before admission. Alternately, institutions can also avail the services of credential evaluation agencies to determine degree equivalencies as well as certify the authenticity of transcripts. Please refer to chapter 6 on credential evaluation for more details on such practices.

Given that we live in an era where the number of refugees in the world is at an all-time high, graduate programs must seriously consider admission options for prospective international students who are displaced and no longer have access to their academic records. U.S. universities can play a crucial role in helping such students further their education as they seek to resettle and start a new life in a new country but lack adequate academic documentation. While this is by no means an easy task, institutions can facilitate the process by providing such students with alternatives such as internal testing related to the subject matter they wish to study, one-on-one interviews, pathway programs, etc.

Other Supplemental Materials

In addition to test scores and academic records, many graduate programs require materials such as résumés, personal essays, statements of purpose, or portfolios for admission. Like standardized tests, these requirements are set for all prospective students. When stating international student requirements, it is important to provide clear guidelines, definitions, and instructions regarding such materials to set realistic expectations for international students. This is especially true for prospective students educated in countries where postsecondary admission is based exclusively on performance on national or institutional level tests.

Letters of Recommendation

As with supplemental materials, providing clear instructions on choosing recommenders can be crucial, especially for international students educated in countries where evaluations are not standard practice for admission.

If recommenders are expected to complete their evaluations online, institutions should use simple platforms that are easy to navigate. It is good practice to use a recommendation form that mixes quantitative metrics (e.g., Likert scale) with qualitative ones (e.g., a letter) so that students can be evaluated on a more standardized scale. If the evaluation is purely qualitative it is especially important to provide clear instructions on areas to comment on, such as strengths and weaknesses and depth of knowledge in subject matter. Given that Internet access is frequently limited in some countries and that evaluators may experience difficulty navigating an online platform, U.S. institutions must provide recommenders flexibility to mail in their evaluations if they so choose.

Funding Opportunities

More than 40 percent of all international students pursuing graduate studies in the United States are supported by their institution of study, sponsored either by their government or place of employment, or receive funding from another type of private entity (Institute of International Education 2016).

Since international students do not typically qualify for many types of financial aid, they may need to borrow money, often at high interest rates, to pay for their U.S. graduate degree. While enrollment trends clearly indicate that international graduate students recognize the quality and return on investment of such degrees, university funding can play a critical role in determining which institution they choose to attend. Being upfront about all degree-related expenses and availability of funding (or lack thereof) is good institutional practice when recruiting international students so that they have a realistic understanding of what to expect and are able to plan accordingly.

Many doctoral programs offer all admitted students full or partial funding via research and teaching assistantships. Such funding may be less common, however, for master's and certificate programs. Offering international students some level of scholarship or assistantship incentivizes them to select an institution. Additionally, providing them a resource guide to accessing external scholarships available to international students can be extremely helpful. While these students have the option to seek on-campus work opportunities once they arrive in the United States, it is important that they follow immigration regulations regarding number of acceptable work hours, off-campus employment etc., and are made aware of the implications of violating immigration regulations.

Select international graduate students may also seek admission with full funding from their governments or from sources such as the Fulbright Commission or the Vietnam Education Fund.

Other Admissions Considerations

Working With Faculty

University faculty are critical members of the graduate selection committee, especially for doctoral programs. It is possible that they may be less attuned to the various challenges international students face when applying to U.S. institutions. Admissions personnel play a critical role in helping faculty to bridge this knowledge gap. Before a selection committee convenes, admissions personnel could conduct information sessions to provide a brief overview of the education systems of the students under consideration. This is especially useful if the institution is seeking to actively recruit students from a particular country or region as part of its enrollment strategy. Providing the selection committee written guidelines for factors to consider for specific countries can also be a useful practice to facilitate faculty engagement. Finally, it is valuable to have a professional credential evaluator available to provide additional information regarding degree equivalencies, grading scales, etc.

Effective Communication

International students seeking graduate education in the United States may experience numerous challenges as they navigate an unfamiliar admissions landscape. Good communication strategies can go a long way in easing this experience for such students and ensuring a positive admission experience.

Whether it is an international admissions website that spans undergraduate and graduate admissions, or a graduate admissions website that also caters to prospective international students, ensure that the user interface is easy to navigate across cultures. Providing specific admission requirements for international students, listing academic document requirements by country, translating relevant admission information pages into other languages for high-volume countries, and promoting funding opportunities for international students are some examples of how this can be achieved.

Besides webinars or in-person sessions that focus on showcasing programs, institutions could also post short videos on admission requirements, common mistakes that prospective international students make, as well as tips on completing the admission process successfully.

It is important to provide students with an application system that is easy to navigate and use across cultures, perhaps even providing additional country-specific instructions and FAQs based on feedback from prospective students from a particular country or region. The application platform or admissions website could provide checklists to guide international students about what they should do before, during, and after submitting their application. This could help set realistic expectations for the admission process.

Postadmission Experiences

At many U.S. institutions, lines can be blurry in determining when the responsibilities of the admissions office ends and when those of other student services kick in. At the very least, it is important for graduate admissions offices to successfully transition admitted students to enroll at their institution. After an international student is admitted and commits to attend an institution, admissions officers can serve as student advocates and can play an important role in helping them navigate next steps prior to their arrival on campus.

Acceptance letters should provide students with clear guidelines about how to certify their enrollment at the institution (e.g., complete a form, pay a commitment deposit, etc.). Students should also be provided with adequate information regarding their conditions of admission, how to satisfy them, and the consequences of not fulfilling these conditions in a timely manner. It is important for international students to have all the information they require beforehand when they are deciding to choose an institution.

Conclusion

Institutions that succeed in attracting international graduate students usually have in place many of the practices referenced in this chapter. Besides having a comprehensive enrollment management strategy, it is also important that U.S. institutions are truly supportive of international students they are seeking to recruit by providing them with adequate information during the admissions process, having open communication with them, and making sure to be culturally sensitive to their academic backgrounds.

References

Council of Graduate Schools. 2015. International Graduate Applications and Enrollment: Fall 2015. http://cgsnet.org/international-graduate-admissions-survey.

Institute of International Education. 2016. *Open Doors Report on International Educational Exchange.* http://www.iie.org/Research-and-Publications/Open-Doors#.WFCvw_krJPY.

6 Foreign Credential Evaluation

By Aleksander Morawski

International credential evaluation is a task faced by any U.S. institution admitting applicants who completed any portion of their prior academic study in a non-U.S. education system. Foreign education systems are diverse in many ways including structure, content, documentation, and outcomes. While in many cases, there is little linearity with the U.S. system of education, the basic principles of credential evaluation can be relied upon to determine an applicant's suitability for your institution, regardless of the academic level or institution type. This chapter will first outline the fundamental (basic) principles of credential evaluation. Moving forward, it will examine issues of transferring credit, concluding with an overview of issues affecting credential authenticity and a discussion about resources.

Basic Principles

The first thing to understand when evaluating credentials is what is being evaluated. Fundamentally, credentials are just pieces of paper, but the information they convey is crucial in determining an applicant's academic accomplishments. Speaking of the applicant, it is therefore essential to determine that the credentials being evaluated actually belong to the applicant. Although this seems like a basic process, it can be much more difficult if your accompanying application is not thorough. Ensure that this supplemental piece asks for accurate biographical information, an academic history, and self-identification of the credentials submitted for evaluation. Foreign naming conventions, academic calendars and terminology, and transnational factors are just some of the potential sources of confusion when beginning the evaluation process.

Official Documents and Determining Degree Equivalency

Many types of documents can be called academic credentials. Therefore, during the evaluation process, an evaluator must determine whether the credentials in question can be evaluated to meet institutional requirements. This task is commonly referred to as determining if the submitted documents are official. The best approach to this is to determine if said documents are sufficient for application to a similar level of study in the home country. Ask, "What do we require from our domestic applicants?" Depending on the answer, the foreign credentials should meet the same expectations one has of credentials from domestic applicants while being mindful that record-keeping and documentation standards vary among different countries. Official credentials will be issued by the correct entity, meaning simply that they are issued by the office or entity of the institution responsible for official academic records. At most U.S. institutions, this would be the registrar rather than, for example, an academic department. These credentials will be issued in the official language of the institution, but be mindful that many foreign academic institutions are multilingual.[1] In cases when official credentials are not issued in English, it is necessary to ensure the presence of accurate English translations, meeting your organization or department's pre-established policy on foreign language documents. The credentials must also state final results instead of provisional ones. It is not prudent to evaluate credentials that may present information that can be changed at a later time.[2] Upon establishing that the credentials presented are sufficient to evaluate, the next step is to establish an overall academic equivalence.

An academic equivalence does not guarantee an exact assessment of academic aptitude gained by earning that credential. Similarly, two students, having earned the same credential from the same institution in the United States, may have different levels of academic aptitude for success in a future program. The fundamental task of an academic credential evaluator is to quantify an inherently abstract concept while relying on predetermined indicators and ensuring consistency in the process. The process occurs in the following steps: determining the academic level, dissecting the coursework, and comparing them to the U.S. education ladder.

Academic levels of education for this publication can be divided into two parts—secondary and postsecondary. Each category can be subdivided into smaller categories, such as lower and upper secondary, or undergraduate versus graduate. Understanding the levels of education in the home institution as well as in foreign programs is necessary in determining an overall equivalence of a foreign credential.

Strategies for Determining Admissibility: Degree Equivalence

One way to determine levels is to understand educational benchmarks. An educational benchmark can be defined as a credential confirming completion of a level of education and granting access to the next level of education. A U.S. high school diploma is a benchmark credential because it denotes completion of secondary education and grants access to postsecondary education programs.[3] A bachelor's degree can also be viewed as a benchmark credential because it denotes completion of undergraduate education and grants access to graduate-level programs. However, not all benchmarks are created equal. There is no international mandate for educational benchmarks to be awarded for a similar amount of education. As such, in addition to educational benchmarks, evaluators typically count the number of full-time years of study it takes to earn said credential and compare it to what a U.S. student would earn in a similar time frame. This is based on the assumption that full-time study at the same level, no matter where in the world, will impart an equal amount of academic knowledge in the same time frame. Academic years are the most universal time measure used for evaluation, but the same principle applies if counting semesters, trimesters, quarters, etc., ensuring that they are defined in the same way as they are at the home institution.

The U.S. high school diploma, the benchmark of secondary education, is traditionally earned upon completion of 12 years of primary and secondary education. However, in foreign programs, this benchmark can be achieved after 10, 11, 12, 13, or more years depending on the country and time of issue.

While each of these matches the definition of a benchmark, the evaluator must determine if its holder's academic preparation resulting from earning that credential is sufficient for his/her intended purpose. Similarly, the U.S. bachelor's degree traditionally requires four years of full-time study. When a similarly named benchmark degree is earned after two, three, four, or more years, is the applicant's level of academic preparation also different? This question goes beyond determining the equivalence of a credential to the more important function in admissions, which is the determination of applicants' capabilities to succeed in the program to which they are applying.

Making an Informed Admissions Decision

Delving deeper into the foreign academic credential evaluation process, it is not always enough to determine the U.S. equivalence. In order to make an informed admission decision, and to meet pre-established institutional guidelines, it is necessary to quantify the studies of various subjects as the units of measurement at the home institution.[4] Foreign academic credentials quantify academic studies in various ways, using points of reference such as contact hours, maximum marks, foreign credits, etc. Converting such programs to the system used by your institution becomes an exercise of proportions—comparing what is presented on the foreign credential to what would be expected to be earned by a full-time student at your institution.[5] Besides ensuring that an international applicant meets specific admission requirements, you can, at this point, assess an applicant's performance in singular subjects, allowing you to more accurately predict his or her preparation for their intended purpose.

Assessing Academic Performance

Assessing academic performance requires an understanding of the message conveyed by grades. Grading is, in fact, another abstract concept that we attempt to quantify. This is done by isolating the few absolute criteria in any type of assessment system—the highest level of achievement and the lowest level of achievement required to 'pass'.[6] This information is required regardless of grading scale type, whether letter, number, percentage, description, or any combination thereof. Moving forward, it is necessary to identify any perceivable performance categories and match them with the categories contained in the U.S. A–F scale accordingly.[7] Stratification, or categorization of different levels of performance, is frequently included on the credentials themselves. Many resources on international education systems, which are discussed further in this chapter, contain information on performance levels as well as recommendations for conversion to the U.S. grading scale.

The final step in the basic principles of credential evaluation is converting a grade point average (GPA). A GPA is the mathematical average of all grades received, with consideration for the weighting of each course. Unlike overall grades used in foreign systems, a GPA is purely a mathematical average and does not place any arbitrary weighting on specific subjects or terms of study beyond the weighting indicated by the credit values. This is the standard by which domestic students' academic performance is compared, necessitating a similar calculation for a consistent assessment of international applicants.

Making an Informed Placement Determination: Transferring Credit

Transferring postsecondary credit from international academic credentials requires the same type of detailed credential evaluation as for an initial admission decision. In U.S. institutions, this process is typically governed by institutional policy set up by registrars. To be effective, it requires the accurate conversion and quantification of foreign academic coursework to the indigenous system used by your institution. At the postsecondary level, transfer credit is typically granted according to institutional policy for coursework completed at the same level at domestic institutions. The challenge, therefore, is consistency across campus in converting foreign credential outcomes to credits and making transfer recommendations. At least three offices may, at any given time, be involved in evaluation of foreign credentials for transfer credit. The admissions office makes initial recommendations as to the evaluation of foreign transcripts. The registrar, academic department, or another entity working with transfer students may be doing the same thing, while a study abroad office may be evaluating the same course work from U.S. students participating in study abroad programs. This scenario is not uncommon at many U.S. universities, regardless of size. A campuswide policy on the evaluation of foreign credentials or a centralized credential evaluation process are two strategies for ensuring consistency.

International transfer credit is further complicated by the fact that levels of education are not linear and overlap with different levels in the U.S. system. The most common issue that arises is the dilemma of postsecondary-level credit for secondary-level course work. It is not uncommon for institutions to grant university-level credit for course work completed beyond the 12th year of full-time study, even if it was completed at a level of education designated as secondary by the home institution.

There is no universal recommendation on transfer credit for such programs. Rather, institutional autonomy provides academic institutions in the United States with the ability to make independent decisions, minding the best interests of their students and their academic programs. As such, determining transferability of credit across academic levels becomes an exercise of course work analysis beyond credential evaluation, requiring consultation of subject matter experts including faculty members who will be teaching these prospective applicants. Of course, the U.S. education system is not excepted from complex transfer credit issues. One needs to look no further than pre-established policies on Advanced Placement or International Baccalaureate programs, which most institutions already have in place, for an example of transfer credit across academic levels.

In summary, transferring credit is a complex process. It begins with consistently thorough and accurate credential evaluation, but affects many stakeholders beyond the admissions office including registrars, academic faculty, study abroad offices, prospective applicants, and current students themselves. As such, one of the most important aspects in the process becomes consistency: consistency in the application of evaluation policies on campus, consistency with transferring credit across university offices, and consistency with peer institutions.

Documentation Considerations

Having discussed the principles of the evaluation process and of utilizing the information for admission decisions and transfer credit, it is time once again to discuss the credentials themselves in light of establishing an effective and efficient evaluation process. Documents can be submitted in various ways. Many domestic admissions processes utilize sophisticated document clearinghouse methods such as electronic submission and storage to effectively manage the volume of domestic application materials. At this time, this is not possible for international applicants who face challenges of access to and availability of documents to submit via clearinghouse methods. Institutional policies should strive for fairness in the application process and to protect the integrity of the process from the possibility of forgery and fraud.

Forgery and fraud in the higher education community are not new concepts. They exist as long as there is the idea of purported personal gain from misrepresentation of academic achievement. Credential evaluators, therefore, have the additional task of combatting this phenomenon in order to protect their institution, their professional integrity, and even those applicants who seek admission to programs for which they are inadequately prepared. Technological advancements have made combatting these issues more effective, but also present new challenges in detecting malice in the admissions process. The first step in combatting forgery and fraud is further analysis of what is being evaluated.

The potential for unintended alteration varies depending on how credentials are submitted. The most secure document submission requirement is to request original credentials to be sent directly by the issuing institution to your office.[8] The reason for this very common requirement is to prevent the credentials from being handled by the applicant. While this is typically the most secure method of document submission, it can present the most challenges due to costs, processing time, and staff availability among many other factors. Upon establishing that it is not possible to receive documents directly from the issuing institution, one may request sealed original documents to be submitted by the applicant. If this is also impossible, the credential evaluator may elect to work with unsealed originals, or with photocopies, submitted directly or electronically.[9] Each method of submission carries a higher risk of potential alteration. However, given application deadlines as well as various factors affecting the availability of credentials from various places, the process must remain flexible in order to equally serve adequately prepared applicants regardless of their origin.

Involving others in the credential evaluation process is an effective way of solving problems of questionable documentation or lack of availability of documents to be sent directly. Establishing relationships with institutions sending larger volumes of students to the United States can expedite the verification process of questionable credentials. However, even without established relationships, it is not beyond the scope of an evaluator's job to request verification of credentials from issuing institutions. It is, after all, in the best interest of institutions to provide this service because it is damaging to an institution's reputation when individuals' (forged) credentials do not match their academic aptitude. The verification process often requires patience, persistence, and research, but more efficient processes are emerging at several institutions across the globe.

Internal and External Resources

Of all the considerations and factors to consider in credential evaluation, two questions remain: who, and how. Identifying the appropriate office or individual at an institution responsible for credential evaluation depends on the size and structure of the institution. The staff considerations vary from one-person offices to dedicated departments for international credential evaluation. However, one of the themes throughout this chapter has been the need for consistency in the process, and this must be emphasized regardless of the institutional structure and size. The ideal way of ensuring this is to maintain a universally accessible and regularly reviewed institutional policy for international credential evaluation. Beyond a stated policy, anyone involved in the process needs access to resources.

Resources on international comparative education systems are published and updated regularly by entities such as foreign ministries of education, organizations like NAFSA and AACRAO, and private credential evaluation firms, to name a few. Although many such resources are accessible for free online, it is prudent to designate funding to invest in commonly used resources, memberships, as well as for continued training and professional development. Education systems are dynamic. Therefore, credential evaluation training, resource review, and professional development of evaluation staff are essential and ongoing processes.

Many academic institutions evaluate international credentials in house. Others outsource the process to private agencies dedicated to the evaluation of foreign academic documents for academic purposes as well as licensure, immigration, and employment. The decision to outsource the process is a complicated one, as your institution is relinquishing the control over a key aspect of the application review process. However, utilizing a service provider with extensive experience and resources can be an efficient solution and result in more accurate evaluation, especially if your institution's resources are limited. There is no governmental oversight for private credential evaluation agencies or a universal mandate to follow any established guidelines. Therefore, the selection of a service provider must be done with care, ensuring a thorough understanding of that provider's policies, requirements, and standards. Two associations, Association of International Credential Evaluators (AICE) and National Association of Credential Evaluation Services (NACES), maintain rigorous selection criteria, codes of conduct, and guidelines for operation, certifying to the operational ethics of member evaluation agencies. Regardless of whether the evaluation is performed internally or outsourced to a third party, haphazard policies and underdeveloped processes pertaining to the evaluation of foreign credentials may result in the admitting institution turning down excellent students while admitting ones who are inadequately prepared for academic success.

Conclusion

Accurate and efficient foreign credential evaluation is an inherent part of the international admissions process. The complexity of the task can be as varied as foreign credentials themselves and is dependent on the purpose of the admission review. The importance of each principle of credential evaluation holds value regardless of the intended purpose because the goal of foreign credential evaluation is consistent with the goal of making effective admission decisions—to admit international students who are adequately prepared to succeed in the programs to which they are applying.

Resources

The resources below are a small sample of major resources on credential evaluation and comparative education systems available to international educators and to the public:

Online

These online resources represent easily accessible, country-specific information on the majority of foreign educational systems. Each profile is authored by subject experts, and is regularly updated.

AACRAO – American Association of Collegiate Registrars and Admissions Officers (AACRAO)
EDGE Database
http://edge.aacrao.org

NAFSA's Online Guide to Educational Systems Around the World
https://www.nafsa.org/ges

Publications (general)

These publications are a collection of evaluation methodologies and country-specific information on education systems and higher education institutions around the world.

Feagles, Shelley M. (Ed.) 1999. *A Guide to Educational Systems Around the World.* Washington, DC: NAFSA: Association of International Educators.

International Association of Universities. 2016. *International Handbook of Universities 2017.* Palgrave Macmillan UK. https://www.nafsa.org/Shop/detail.aspx?id=136E

Freeman, Kathleen. 2016. *Evaluating Foreign Educational Credentials.* Washington, DC: NAFSA: Association of International Educators. https://www.nafsa.org/Shop/detail.aspx?id=136E

The New Country Index Volume 1 and 2. International Education Research Foundation, 2004; 2011.

Publications (country-specific)

Such publications offer detailed descriptions of a country's education systems.

China, Country Report, PIER World Education Series. 2000. Washington, DC: AACRAO and NAFSA.

Feagles, Shelley M. 2008. *Tools for Evaluating Educational Documents from Vietnam*. Milwaukee: ECE Insights.

Wenger, Margaret L. 2012. *The Kingdom of Saudi Arabia: Its Educational System and Methods of Evaluation*. Milwaukee: ECE Presents.

Endnotes

[1] It is increasingly common for foreign institutions to issue official documents in English as well as in the native language. Although it can be expected that academic documents should be available in the native language, it may present undue difficulty and expense for an applicant to submit native language documents when those issued in English serve a similar purpose. Further investigation of the institution's practices is necessary to correctly determine if non-native language documentation can be considered official.

[2] Due to application deadlines, it may become necessary to make admissions decisions and placement recommendations based on provisional results, in cases when final certificates are not issued in time for applicants to meet application deadlines. In such scenarios, an institutional policy must be in place to ensure that final, official credentials match those on which the decision was made.

[3] A U.S. high school diploma grants access to open enrollment postsecondary programs such as those in community colleges. More selective institutions have more specific admissions requirements. However, since any high school diploma can provide access to some form of postsecondary education, it can be viewed as a benchmark.

[4] Most common units of study at U.S. institutions are Carnegie units for secondary-level programs and semester credits or quarter credits for postsecondary programs.

[5] Common expected semester credit totals for undergraduate programs in the United States: 15 credits/semester; 30 credits/1 year; 120 credits/4 years.

[6] Coursework only evaluated on a pass/fail basis, without different degrees of performance, should not be assigned a letter grade or counted in a GPA.

[7] The lowest passing grade in the United States is typically a D for secondary-level programs, C for undergraduate postsecondary programs, and B for graduate-level programs. It is highly recommended to consult your institutional grading scale and convert foreign grades accordingly.

[8] Even documents sent directly by the issuing institutions are not immune from 'inside job' fraud when corrupt officials, employed by academic institutions, intentionally send inauthentic academic credentials for students, usually in exchange for payment. If, upon a holistic review of an application, the credentials are not congruent with the rest of the application, further investigation may be required.

[9] Many institutions that evaluate a large volume of international transcripts allow for electronic submission of documents by applicants or self-reporting of their results, with the caveat of conditions being placed on admission that original documents are submitted prior to registration.

7 Managing an International Admissions Office

By Matthew R. Beatty

In an era of increasing competition for international students, evolving immigration regulations, and limited institutional resources, enrollment managers must demonstrate the ability to reach measurable outcomes that stakeholders value and expect. As a result, the importance of a highly efficient, student-focused, and outcome-oriented international admissions office has never been greater than it is today. In this chapter, the author applies an existing framework in an effort to manage quality, accuracy, and efficiency throughout the entire international admissions process.

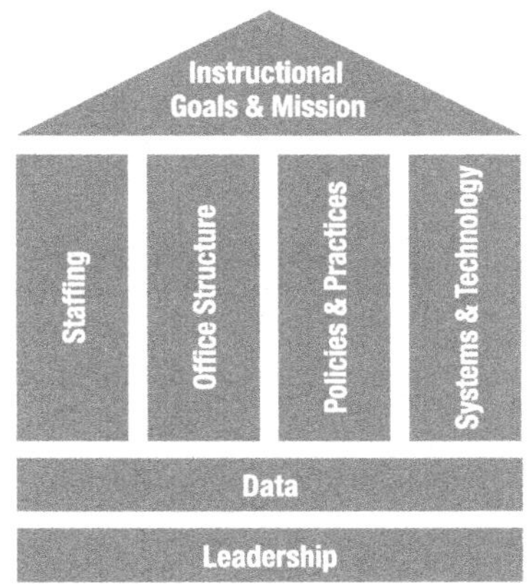

Figure 1: Seven Components of an Effective Admissions Office

Image reproduced with permission from Karl Stumo.

Figure 1 reflects seven critical components of a highly effective admissions organization. The concept was designed by Karl Stumo, vice president of enrollment and marketing at Concordia College, and is comprised of institutional goals and mission, staffing, office structure, policies and practices, systems and technology, data, and leadership. While your institution may benefit from advancement within each of these areas, the sum of these seven components, effectively applied, are greater than the individual parts. These components are intended to be interrelated and inseparable. This chapter focuses on these seven components within the context of managing an international admissions office.

Institutional Goals and Mission

While the requirements for international applicants may differ slightly from domestic students, the overarching goal-setting process remains the same. Successful organizations involve key institutional stakeholders while setting realistic goals pertaining to international admission (Sigler 2007). Enrollment goals need to be based on philosophy, values, and empirical data shared among institutional leaders. Measurable outcomes and designated time frames must be also determined. To begin the process, some international admissions managers will conduct an institutional self-study, develop a plan of action, and recognize potential enrollment challenges and opportunities. When performed successfully, everyone involved will be able to understand their roles and allocate resources to achieve the expected outcomes. They will also be able to answer critical questions pertaining to international enrollment management (IEM) on campus.

Merit- and need-based financial aid goals should also be established at the outset since international students are ineligible to receive U.S. federal financial aid. While some international students have the means to pay full tuition rates, many prospective students and their families seek financial assistance at the undergraduate, graduate, and even English language program levels.

Critical Questions for IEM Goal Setting:

- Why are international students important to your institution?
- What is the institution's international enrollment goal?
- What, if any, enrollment targets are there for individual countries, markets, or academic quality?
- To achieve desired results, what types of performance benchmarks must be accomplished at pivotal junctions of the enrollment funnel?
- Have strategies to achieve the desired goals been clearly outlined?
- What financial aid program(s) exist to support new internationals students?

Staffing

The heart of any great organization is its staff and the special regard they have for their workplace. The dedication, positive outlook, and *esprit de corps* of a well-managed admissions team have the potential to overcome even the most daunting enrollment challenges. This is the first and most critical pillar for managing a successful admissions office as reflected in Figure 1.

Developing a highly efficient international admissions office requires staff training, diligence, and a sense of humor. Formal cross-cultural awareness and comparative education training can be an effective way to improve the productivity of an inexperienced team. Recruiters need to learn about different communication styles and cultural norms to counsel prospective students. Credential evaluators must have access to information on educational systems and transfer credits from outside of the United States. Processing staff may need support to accurately interpret and input personal data into a student information database. Ideally, managers provide all staff with opportunities to acquire and strengthen their professional competencies while working in a multicultural setting. Furthermore, they should provide individual feedback and a clear direction of where the unit is heading.

NAFSA's International Education Professional Competencies™ publication describes the necessary skill sets for all international education domains including international enrollment management. This is an excellent resource when hiring new employees, creating job descriptions, and identifying areas for further staff development. For a copy of the NAFSA International Education Professional Competencies™, visit http://www.nafsa.org/competencies.

Maintaining morale and efficiency throughout the admissions process can be difficult, especially when responding to the unique needs of international students. Therefore, it is important that staff have opportunities to learn fresh recruitment tactics, expand their institutional knowledge base, and sharpen their foreign credential evaluation skills. Plus, the chance to network with colleagues and gain critical insight about evolving admissions standards can make a processing season less stressful. The professional development opportunities within the field of international admissions and enrollment management are boundless.

Structure

The second pillar of Stumo's diagram relates to the organizational structure and responsibilities of an admissions office. Traditionally, domestic and international admissions offices have been set up within a U.S. college or university's division of enrollment management. In this scenario, directors of domestic and international admissions report to the same senior administrator for student services, often a vice president or assistant provost for enrollment management. However, within the context of the international unit, there really is no typical office structure. Depending on the institution's size and volume of applications, the international admissions unit may be comprised of one or many staff members who are responsible for global outreach, recruitment, application processing, admissions, financial aid, and marketing.

For a variety of reasons, a growing number of U.S. institutions are repositioning some or all of their international admissions functions to offices outside of their enrollment management division. Some institutions have relocated international recruitment and admission responsibilities into the Office of International Affairs. Other large universities have adopted a hybrid approach whereby empowering individual departments and international service offices to recruit students abroad while retaining core admission functions within their Office of Admissions. Another set of institutions employ third-party providers to manage all aspects of their international recruitment, admissions, and outreach operations.

Whatever the organizational structure might look like, it is imperative that college and university leaders have carefully assessed and addressed areas of administrative efficiency, accountability, and fiscal management so they can justify operational changes. Table 1 outlines some of the advantages and disadvantages of four international admissions office structures.

Table 1: International Admissions Office Structures

Structure	Advantages	Disadvantages
Domestic and International Admissions Model: Domestic and international student recruitment, admissions, and marketing functions are shared within the same office.	• One chain of command • Shared staff and marketing resources • Synthesized enrollment reports • Streamlined data processing and student information system processes	• Susceptible to one-size-fits-all application model • Often heavily focused on domestic students • Promotional material may not be culturally appropriate for international students
International Admission and Services Model: International admissions and service operations are housed within the institution's Office of International Affairs.	• Accountability over all aspects of IEM • Greater institutional consistency when interpreting immigration regulations • Specialized focus toward international admissions and student services • Fosters immediate integration of new students with current international programs and services	• Separate administrative reporting lines • May cause confusion among prospective applicants and visitors • Requires additional resources to unify institutional brand, marketing material, and reports
Decentralized International Admissions Model: International recruitment and admission operations are housed within individual departments or graduate programs.	• Allows schools and departments to customize recruitment and admissions efforts • Reduces bureaucratic layers	• Requires additional resources and training • Duplication of efforts and resources • Difficult to manage changes to admission policies and standards • May cause confusion among applicants
Third-Party Partnership Model: International recruitment and admissions procedures are managed exclusively by a private, third-party provider.	• High level of international education expertise • Increased levels of efficiency • Enhanced access to new student markets	• Costly • Limited institutional control • Possible conflict of institutional vision

Practices and Policies

Preserving institutional integrity and accuracy throughout the international admissions process requires well-documented policies and practices. This constitutes the third pillar in Stumo's diagram. Inconsistencies in the evaluation of foreign credentials and mishandling of student records are not only embarrassing, but can also be detrimental to an institution's reputation, and enrollment outcomes may suffer. Therefore, it is imperative that staff make concerted efforts to review, revise, and record internal business practices. Simultaneously, it is important to remember that each student case is unique and may require some level of professional discretion. Figure 2 offers several strategies to improve the integrity of the review while engaging students throughout the various steps of the enrollment process within the framework of a modified enrollment funnel.

Figure 2: Strategies to Maintain Admissions Integrity Throughout Enrollment Funnel

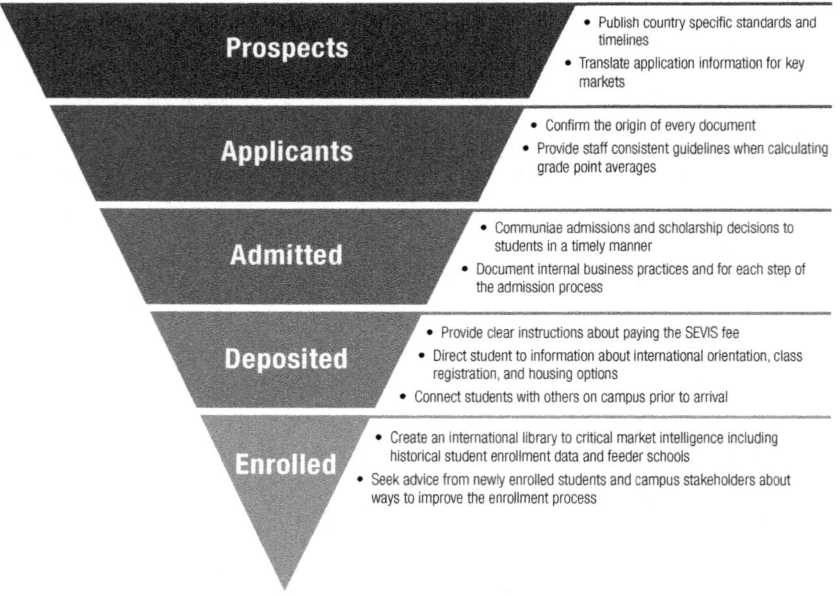

Institutions may also experience unanticipated complications when admitting international students. These complications slow down institutional momentum and can introduce new risks for the university. As defined by Pamela Barrett, CEO of Barton Carlyle, strategic risk is "any substantive risk which is an existential threat to either the international programs at institution, or the institution as a whole" (Bowman 2015). Strategic risk may include the acceptance of falsified academic documentation, over-reliance on one student market, and approval of fraudulent financial records. These risks pose challenges to admissions practices and delay desired outcomes. Drafting admissions policies to address potential risks reduces exposure, expedites training time for new staff members, and communicates consistent protocols when handling similar yet distinct student cases. Figure 3 includes a series of policy-related questions worth considering at various points of the enrollment process.

Figure 3: Policy Questions Pertaining to International Admissions

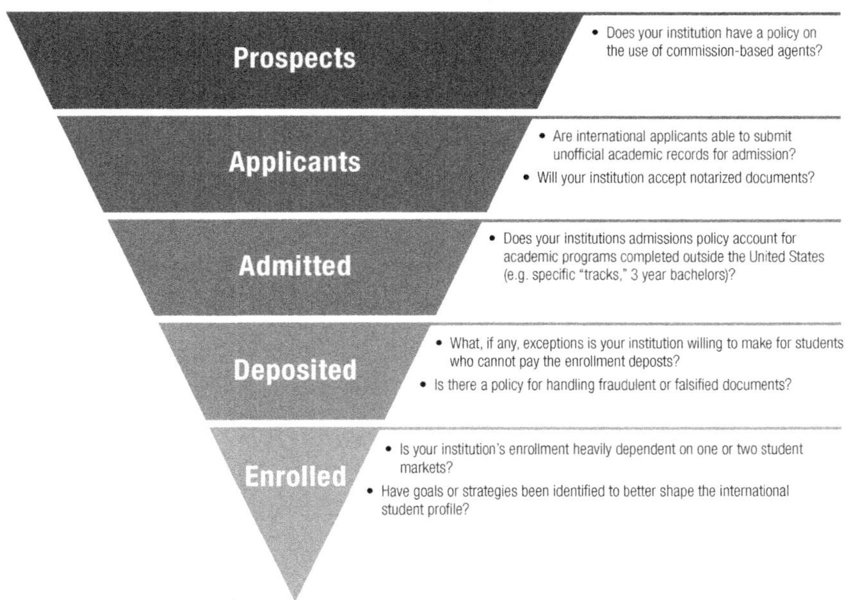

Systems and Technology

The fourth pillar of Stumo's diagram refers to systems and technology as they relate to enrollment management. Technology has introduced higher education to an era of immense data, increased globalization, and access to information at lightening quick speeds. According to Wayne John Brown in an article for Educause, to remain competitive institutions must align with trends in technology and leverage institutional systems in order to be part of the virtual community student's desire. In the context of global admissions, this equates to emerging opportunities to communicate with students and the demand of greater transparency throughout the admissions process.

As noted by Elizabeth White, assistant director of international admissions at the University of Buffalo:

> The development of more sophisticated student information systems has given admission officers better tools with which to admit applicants and then track those admitted students through their university careers. Online applications dump applicant information into these systems, reducing staff time devoted to data entry. These systems, in turn, feed data warehouses, which give easier access to information about application, allowing for better trend analysis. (White 2010)

The ideal scenario would be a student information system that allows staff from various units to neatly track individual applicant behavior, and capture correspondences as well as the completion of standard business operations in a user-friendly fashion. Simultaneously, it would relay clear, concise, and relevant information to appropriate students and stakeholders in a timely manner. In reality, not every office is able to afford or harness the power of cutting-edge technologies—nor should they. The key is to find an adaptable yet affordable suite of processing and communication technologies that interface with your campus's student information system efficiently while meeting the majority of your students' expectations.

Ensure that the suite can be adequately managed by an international admissions team with the support of campus IT. An integrated system of this nature guarantees the greatest chance of achieving an institution's enrollment goals. Anything less leads to wasted time, efforts, and money for both the admissions office and the student.

Whichever technologies, social media platforms, and information systems your institution chooses, it is strongly recommended that admissions offices maintain a student-centered approach. This involves seeking feedback about the admissions experience from current students. Ask them questions about their interactions with the program's application. Conduct focus groups to learn more about their preferred communications methods. Ultimately, the more information you have about the student experience and related expectations, the more informed you will be while considering future systems and technologies.

Data

At the foundation of a highly effective international admissions office rests empirical data. Until recently, international admissions offices have struggled to present empirical and outcome-based data. Thankfully, as White alluded to previously, new advancements in student information systems have allowed admissions offices to more carefully track student behavior and international application workflows. As an increasing number of U.S. institutions are investing more heavily in IEM, their leadership has demanded corporate-like justification for the money spent to attract, admit, and retain new students. This means accountability throughout the international admissions process is paramount. Not only do recruiters need to develop a solid sense for what's working and what's not, but managers must also be able to measure staff performances and identify bottlenecks within the admissions process (Darrup Boychuck 2009).

As best practice, it is recommended that managers track processing times to complete core functions within the admissions workflow. This includes determining how long it takes to review an application, render an admission decision, and create an admission packet including the student's initial Form I-20 or Form DS-2019. Consistently tracking these types of timelines allows managers to control optimal performance standards. Monitoring keys phases of the admissions operation also enables managers to locate processing delays and identify solutions to improve operations during peak periods of the admissions season.

Looking beyond ordinary operational reports, it is essential that office managers have access to reliable institutional data so they can spot academic trends within their admissions pool. Reliable data can also identify gaps of information and inform future decisions concerning program standards, transfer credit policies, and application timelines. Without this type of outcome-oriented data, admissions officers may never be able to validate their work for the university administration and may not achieve critical enrollment goals. Several examples of this information may include:

- Weekly reports comparing the number of international applications, admission decisions, and enrollment figures from one year to the next.
- Weekly reports comparing the academic performances of various cohorts. Reflecting overall student GPAs, average TOEFL scores, SAT/ACT results, and similar performance indicators.
- "Point in time" reports reflecting the conversion rates at each prospective student stage.

Leadership

Leadership is the final component to a successful and outcome-oriented admissions office and the base for Stumo's diagram. Leadership is about providing the vision and focus to determine where the institution is headed, who it is serving, what outcomes the institution stakeholders value and expect, and how it can stay relevant as conditions change (Kotter 1990). These same leadership characteristics carry over into the other six components.

Long-term international admissions success begins with a commitment from university and college leadership. It includes a clear statement from the president or Board of Regents, defining the institution's rationale for enrolling foreign students, and states specific goals regarding their enrollment. The statement should acknowledge that students from different cultures and educational systems require advice and assistance that must be organized and funded by the host institution. Corresponding academic policies and student programs related to the enrollment of international students should be directly related to the institution's mission statement and goals.

While the vision to actively enroll international students may start at the institution's highest level, the implementation process can be strenuous. It requires ongoing collaboration and communication by a variety of campus leaders. Gauging the campus's willingness, readiness, and ability to achieve this presidential objective is essential. This means international admissions offices must have a clear understanding of the institution's culture and resources available to serve students once they arrive. Strong working relationships among international student advisers, orientation leaders, residence life directors, dining services managers, and academic support staff are pivotal. After all, individual managers from these areas will ultimately be expected to solve a dynamic set of internal and external factors affecting enrollment goals (Sinclair 2010).

Conclusion

In summary, your office and perhaps even your institution may temporarily benefit from progress with each of the seven components described in this chapter. However, managing a successful international admissions office often necessitates continuous, transformative change. Administering substantive change among the sum of these seven interconnected components requires participation by many contributors—including champions for international enrollment who may be situated outside of the admissions office.

References

Bowman, Karen Doss. 2015. "Managing Strategic Risk in International Enrollment Management." *International Educator* 24, 2:50. https://www.nafsa.org/_/File/_/ie_julaug15_enrollment.pdf.

Brown, Wayne John. 2014. "How IT Can Support Student Recruitment (and Why It Should)." *EDUCAUSE review*, January 27, 2014. http://er.educause.edu/articles/2014/1/how-it-can-support-student-recruitment-and-why-it-should.

Darrup Boychuck, Cheryl. 2009. "Measuring Results." *NAFSA's Guide to International Student Recruitment, 2nd Edition*. Washington, DC: NAFSA: Association of International Educators.

Kotter, John. 1990. *A Force for Change: How Leadership Differs from Management.* New York: Free Press.

Sigler, Wayne. 2007. *Managing for Outcomes: Shifting from Process-Centric to Results-Oriented Operations*. Washington, DC: American Association of Collegiate Registrars and Admissions Officers.

Sinclair, Julie. 2010. *International Enrollment Management: Framing the Conversation*. Washington, DC: NAFSA: Association of International Educators.

White, Elizabeth. 2010. "Technology in International Admissions." Ed. D. Williams, R. Watkins and M. Baxton. *The AACRAO International Guide: A Resource for International Education Professionals*. Washington, DC: American Association of Collegiate Registrars and Admissions Officers.

8 PART A
Bridge and Pathway Programs

By Peter Baker

As international student enrollment in the United States has increased, admissions options to accommodate their respective academic needs have also grown. Traditionally, "full enrollment" (to take credit-bearing courses) and "conditional enrollment" (to study English) were the admission types universities had at their disposal. An entire demographic of international students wasn't being accommodated by those options, however, so bridge and pathway programs were developed and are increasingly being offered autonomously by institutions or in partnership with third-party providers. While readers may be aware that the U.S. Department of Homeland Security's Student and Exchange Visitor Program (SEVP) uses "pathway program" as an umbrella term that includes bridge programs, this chapter makes a clear distinction between the two so as to highlight key similarities and differences in how they are typically structured from an academic standpoint.

At their core, these programs are options for students whose English language proficiency levels are between that which is appropriate for an English language learner and a student who is eligible for full admission. Students in these programs take credit-bearing courses to improve the English language proficiency level, and lower-level regular credit-bearing courses. From the perspective of many institutions, they are attractive options to increase international student enrollment. A myriad of marketing, advising, academic, and administrative components that are necessary for these programs to be financially viable, however, must be taken into consideration before the significant decision to develop and offer these programs is made.

Final policy guidance published by SEVP defines a pathway program for reason of English proficiency as "A postsecondary program of study combining credit-bearing and developmental ESL coursework to prepare a student who is unable to meet the English proficiency standards for admission. Such a program leads into an SEVP-certified degree program" (U.S. Department of Homeland Security 2016, 2).

Students interested in pathway programs generally intend to pursue degrees at U.S. institutions of higher education after addressing the item (or items) that prevent them from achieving full admission. By far, the biggest factor that these students must address is a deficient English language proficiency level. The durations of these programs can vary, but year-long options are the most common.

Table 1: Curricular and Advising Elements for Pathway Programs

Typical First-Semester Elements	Typical Second-Semester Elements
• Credit-bearing intensive English language courses • One regular term/credit-bearing mathematics or symbolic systems (e.g., computer science) course • An English language proficiency exam at the end of the first semester	• A full load of lower-level regular term/credit-bearing courses aligned to the student's respective intended academic major to satisfy prerequisite and general education requirements • An English language proficiency exam at the end of the second semester (even if the necessary score for full admission was achieved at the end of the first semester)

Students should receive intensive advising throughout the program to track progress and identify necessary academic and support services interventions if necessary. If done effectively, pathway programs can lead to high rates of matriculation from conditional to full admission, and persistence to graduation.

Like pathway programs, bridge programs provide a means for students in the same situation—deficient English language proficiency score—to take credit-bearing courses. Unlike pathway program students, however, these students do not intend to graduate from the host U.S. university; they instead wish to transfer credits to their home institution and/or just have the experience of taking regular classes at a U.S. university. Curricular and advising elements for bridge programs may include:

- Noncredit intensive English language courses during the duration of the program (usually one semester);
- One or two regular, credit-bearing lower-level courses;
- An English language proficiency exam at the end of the program; and
- Intensive advising throughout the program—to track progress, employ academic interventions, etc.

Students in bridge programs are generally responsible for identifying the credit-bearing classes they'd like to take during their time in the program to have transferred to count toward their degree requirements at their home institution. The bridge program adviser, however, should help to facilitate that process and explain the program to academic units if they are reluctant to admit the students, since they are still conditionally admitted.

Both of these programs are different from dual- or joint-degree programs because, among other considerations, they usually don't require credit transfer articulation agreements between institutions. In both bridge and pathway programs, students receive a diploma from one institution. If they wish to transfer credits, as many bridge program students intend, that process is administered at the individual student level rather than between institutions. Bridge and pathway programs join full (or unconditional) and conditional admission, and dual and joint degrees, as admission and program options that institutions can administer to accommodate international students.

Within the past several years, these programs have become increasingly common and are either offered autonomously by the respective institution or in partnership with a third-party provider. The terms of those partnerships vary but usually include the provider recruiting on behalf of the university it partners with, hiring staff who work at the partner university to conduct administrative and advising services, and a contract period of long duration. International student sponsors are increasingly recognizing the utility of these programs (especially if the students they support are degree-seeking), so program administrators should not limit their recruitment efforts to direct recruitment.

Building and Managing Bridge and Pathway Programs

Bridge and pathway programs have a much more intensive interface with an institution's academic infrastructure than English language programs. Essential requirements to offer these programs, which might push institutions to accommodate students in new ways, include the ability for students who aren't fully admitted to take credit-bearing courses, and for courses exclusively intended to improve English language proficiency levels to be offered for credit. Because of the relative academic importance and newness of these requirements, it is essential to have buy-in for these programs from leadership. To achieve this, the institution's senior international officer (SIO) should introduce bridge and pathway programs to the chief academic officer and other academic and administrative officers. In that presentation, the SIO should stress that similar programs have been established at peer institutions, and explain how they will be administered and the probable enrollment benefit. Only after awareness and consensus at this level is reached should their development start in earnest.

Other stakeholders that must be partnered with along the way, and some of the functions they'll serve, include but are not limited to:

- **Academic Units:** These programs cannot be offered without the consent and participation of academic programs. Remember that they are individualized to the intended major of the respective student. A typical format for a year-long pathway program, for example, is during the first semester that students take credit-bearing English language developmental courses, then in the second regular credit-bearing classes to satisfy general education requirements and/or prerequisites for the respective major. The academic units should tell the (bridge and pathway) program administrators what lower prerequisite courses students should take. Additionally, students in the program should start meeting with faculty members in their departments, and participate in other activities such as related student clubs. This engagement is an effective way to achieve increased retention rates.

- **Admissions:** Students in these programs will not be fully admitted, and usually they are conditionally admitted. In the student's letter of acceptance, however, it should clearly state that he or she is admitted to the bridge or pathway program; if a student in the pathway program has an intended major, his or her admission letter and admission status in the system can be "admitted to the *** (academic program name) pathway program." Additionally, the online and hard-copy international student application should have an option for these programs.
- **Advising:** Intensive advising is absolutely essential for these programs to be successful. The programs' advisers must make sure the students are enrolled in the appropriate courses and make sure they're making progress at the rate necessary to achieve full admission (for pathway program students). This means there must be multiple advising meetings per academic term, and institutions must determine where these advisers will be administratively located—the undergraduate advising office, international student and scholar services office, the intensive English language program, or somewhere else? Wherever they're located, these advisers must have access to the entire academic spectrum of the institution, from English language instructors to academic advisers to faculty.
- **Business Services:** These programs typically have unique tuition and fee structures, and are usually run with cost-recovery budgets. Because of this, the business services office will need to build new student bill models, and route revenue to the respective academic and administrative units. Program costs vary, but usually they are less than nonresident rates. Students would pay the standard, nonresident rate after they matriculate from the program to full admission.

- **English as a Second Language (ESL) experts:** Both programs have the shared objective to provide alternate academic and enrollment options to students whose ability lands between that of an English language learner and one who is prepared for full admission. The minimum English proficiency level necessary to participate in these programs, therefore, must be thoughtfully considered. In consultation with ESL experts, the typical proficiency gains within the duration of the program must be considered to establish the minimum level necessary for admission to the programs. That is, if the program is one academic year in duration, what is the typical gain of English language proficiency for a student who participates in its curriculum? Whatever that typical gain is should be deducted from the level for full admission and serve the minimum requirement for admission. That being said, remember that these programs don't necessarily need to be one academic year in duration, and multiple tracks within the same program can be offered (e.g., options for one semester- and one academic year-long pathway programs).
- **Extension College:** Bridge programs are generally administratively less complicated pathways as their English language courses aren't for credit. Pathway programs' courses, including those intended to support English language skills development, are offered for credit and should be counted toward a student's total credit load requirement. Because of this, an academic unit is necessary to route the English language courses through to have them count for credit. An institution's Extension College is the most likely partner in this effort.
- **Immigration:** Consult with your institution's PDSO and RO to make sure the programs don't violate any rules that govern your participation in the F-1 and J-1 programs. Pay special attention to your institution's Form I-17 to make sure you're eligible and approved to offer SEVIS certified pathway programs.
- **Recruitment:** Institutions obviously need to market these programs. Because these will be new programs, train up your recruitment

team—especially about the admission requirements. Recruiters should use these programs as tools to individualize their conversations with prospective students, to demonstrate that the institution has multiple options for them and not just English language study or full admission.

- **Registrar:** The registrar's office must build the mechanisms to code students who are admitted to these programs to allow them to take credit-bearing courses even though they won't be fully admitted.

Efficiency and Sustainability

Before deciding to build these programs, conduct a market analysis to ensure enough international students would enroll in them to achieve financial viability in the relatively short period of time (2-3 years). During that investigation, remember that just because your institution might offer an intensive English language program that doesn't necessarily mean a bridge or pathway program will be successful. A significant reason why it might be is if your institution also has degree-bearing academic programs that are of interest to international students.

Once the decision has been reached to offer these programs, standardized administrative processes should be established. Don't "overbuild" or excessively individualize the programs; each of their tracks should be quite similar to one another. For a year-long pathway program, for example, pathway students should take the same credit-bearing English language courses regardless of their intended major. In the second semester students start differentiating the classes they take per their intended major. The curricular composition of that second semester should be established in collaboration with the academic department while keeping in mind that the students probably have not achieved full admission—yet—and the courses during that second semester should be those that satisfy general education and the respective program's lower-level prerequisite requirements. To build these tracks, standardized templates should be provided to the academic departments to complete after the programs are introduced.

As previously mentioned, bridge and pathway programs can be offered at either the undergraduate or graduate levels. Due to the differences in the respective admissions processes, however, undergraduate pathway and bridge programs can generally be more expeditiously administered. This is important because the speed by which admission decisions can be reached will significantly impact overall yield (i.e., the more quickly students receive an admission decision the more likely they are to come to the program). Graduate pathway programs, however, require considerably more front-end work to ensure admission decisions can be quickly reached.

Graduate programs have their own admission standards, and pathway and bridge programs should not and will not diminish those standards, if administered correctly. The key to making them work is structured collaboration with the respective graduate programs. That is, meetings should be held with relevant faculty, staff and administrators to introduce the overall concept of pathway and bridge programs, and the respective admission requirements should be built into the programs' tracks in addition to English language proficiency requirements (e.g., if a graduate entrance exam is required support to prepare for it and a date by which results must be submitted should be built into the track). Although bridge programs are possible at the graduate level, pathway programs are far more common.

If an institution is interested in pursuing these programs they can do so autonomously or partner with a third-party provider. There are several providers that generally work with multiple institutions around the world, and especially in the United States, Australia, Canada, and the United Kingdom. They bring expertise in the development, administration, and recruitment for these programs, and seek long-term partnerships with universities. Financial models vary from partnership to partnership, but typically providers recoup the majority of a student's tuition while they are in the respective program; after they matriculate, all revenue goes to the institution. If an institution offers these programs autonomously, it should promote the opportunity to all of its partners—organizations that manage sponsored international student programs, overseas institutional partners, recruitment agents, international students, and others. Refer to NAFSA's "Landscape of Pathway Partnerships in the United States" (see http://www.nafsa.org/Professional_Resources/Browse_by_Interest/International_Students_and_Scholars/Landscape_of_Pathway_Partnerships_in_the_United_States/) for more information.

Universities should familiarize themselves with the various academic and support services that must be coordinated to effectively administer these programs. Even if an institution has the prerequisite resources—an intensive English language program, academic programs that are in high demand by international students, staff that can be tasked to administer and advise the students, etc.—coordinating and marketing these programs is a significant investment. The decision to offer either of these programs, therefore, should not be taken lightly and institutional leadership must express its support clearly and extensively. These programs should not be regarded as secondary considerations in an institution's recruitment strategy—they must be prominently positioned as a top-tier strategy.

Reference

U.S. Department of Homeland Security, Student and Exchange Visitor Program. 2016. SEVP Policy Guidance S7.2: Pathway Programs for Reasons of English Proficiency. https://www.ice.gov/doclib/sevis/pdf/pathwayS7.2englishProficiencyReasons.pdf.

8 PART B

Agents

By Ryan Fleming

Integrating third-party agent activity into the important work of an international admissions unit can be a puzzling, if not daunting, task. On the one hand, having recruitment partners in-country who can generate leads year-round, provide local market insights, and inform institutional strategy through quantitative and qualitative input is an essential component of incorporating agents into a recruitment plan, which is detailed at length in *NAFSA's Guide to International Student Recruitment, Third Edition*. The decision of whether or not to work with agents (while possessing its own complexities) is nonetheless a fairly binary one. On the other hand, it can be less clear how best to engage with agents throughout the international admissions process once the partnership is finalized. Strong communication, high levels of efficiency, and a top-notch student experience are key.

It is this lattermost point that can serve as a proverbial north star when aligning agent partnerships with your international admissions unit. Reputable agents, like reputable higher education institutions (HEIs), are student-centric; the clarity and timeliness of information and updates during the application process will most greatly inform the quality of the student experience—and have the most impact on the student's estimation of your institution. Given the impact a third-party agent can have on your brand and reputation at this stage, collaboration is essential.

As with recruitment, considering third-party agents as an extension of your admissions team entails examining issues of access and authority. HEI adoption of third-party agent partnerships in the United States is approaching 40 percent, still modest when compared with British, Australian, and Canadian peers (Bridge Education Group 2016). While the HEI environments between Anglophone countries are not perfectly analogous, it can be insightful to see what decisions of access and authority between HEIs and agents are made in more mature markets.

At its most extreme, agents can act as extensions of admissions teams in the literal sense, by offering on-the-spot admissions abroad. This strategy is not broadly practiced in the United States, mostly due to regulatory restrictions codified in 8 CFR 214.3(k)(2), which require admissions materials be "received, reviewed, and evaluated at the school's location in the United States" before a Form I-20 or Form DS-2019 can be issued. Avoiding on-the-spot admissions may protect the perceived integrity of the admissions process but comes with disadvantages for efficiency and turnaround times. Still, there are other approaches with more transferability. Consider how you might adopt some of the following practices that are common in peer destination countries:

- Do you operate in-country offices in countries where you are partnered with agents? Are you leveraging this overlap to reduce application decision times? It's important for in-country teams to meet and develop a working rapport. A university representative who shares a culture and time zone with an agent can lend support and confidence to the latter during the application process.
- What is your policy regarding transcript evaluations? Reputable, experienced agents are well acquainted with local educational institutions; leveraging their proximity by empowering them to evaluate and/or certify the authenticity of transcripts, if only on a preliminary basis (subject to the student submitting originals upon arrival to campus) could reduce overall application turnaround time. A quicker decision, in turn, has its own attendant benefits as regards the student's perception of the application experience and your institution as a whole.

- Some UK institutions have different tiers of access for different agents based on market, reputation, and performance. At the highest levels, institutions share information about how foreign universities are assessed and evaluated. While these systems may be strictly internal and assuredly sensitive, consider how collaborating with your top agents could boost efficiency by aligning or perhaps even refining these assessments.
- Does your institution have its own English language assessment? Consider training in-country agent partners to administer these exams and eliminate a layer of bureaucracy for applicants. More broadly, look for ways to simplify this component of the process for your applicants. Ask if your recruitment partners own, operate, or have agreements with English language test centers, which can streamline the student's application journey and boost perceptions of the ease of your application process.
- Have candid discussions about expectations. It's easy for admissions units to feel overwhelmed with agent inquiries soliciting application status updates. Be upfront with your agent partners about processing times across academic levels and departments to reduce frustration or perceptions of unresponsiveness. In the United States, higher education generally and graduate admissions in particular are notoriously decentralized. Agents may not be familiar with this unique aspect of U.S. higher education.

Beyond trimming time and cost, the above initiatives can reduce frustration for genuine students working their way through your application process.

Training is Not a Vaccine

What intake process does your institution have in place for new hires? Can they take a seat at their desks on day one and begin immediately discharging the duties of their position with speed and accuracy? Of course not! Internal additions to the team are owed a credible orientation program and will likely undergo extensive training before they can be truly effective. All too often, however, agents are viewed as mere contractors or creditors instead of valued members of the team. Unsurprisingly, the 2014 Agent Barometer survey revealed that quick response times, a supply of detailed program information, and familiarization trips to partner campuses for training purposes were all top concerns (Coelen 2015).

Upon finalization of a partnership, ensure that there is an "onboarding" experience to get things off on the right foot. Just as a new hire cannot be expected to show up to work on his first day and be immediately productive, so agents too need an onboarding process to be brought up to speed with both high-level information and nitty-gritty details about your institution. Neglecting the onboarding process can have deleterious effects on an agent's ability to file timely, complete applications with confidence. It goes without saying that attention to particular admissions processes and peculiarities should be addressed in training with ample opportunity for question and answer. Beyond these baseline requirements, though, agents would benefit greatly from an onboarding experience that features:

- **A face-to-face meeting, whether in an agent office or on campus.** Personal relationships—in what is perhaps the greatest irony to emerge from the digital age—are more important than ever. At a bare minimum, platforms such as Skype or GoToMeeting allow for some "facetime" and can be a good venue for introducing agent partners to your entire team and other relevant stakeholders on campus. Do your best to ensure that the entire team—from both sides—has a chance to get acquainted. Depending on the size of the agency, there may be regional managers or other contact people with whom you'll be working.
- **Information about the HEI's history and mission.** Counselors who speak to students every day may not be as familiar with your institution as the handful of people who negotiated the contract. It's their turn to hear

your school's story. After all, they'll be expected to retell it on your behalf!

- **Information about the HEI's culture.** Think beyond GPA and test scores. What kind of student excels at your institution? What unique attributes differentiate your institution from others with similar programs and admission requirements? Make sure your training addresses softer issues of institutional "fit." Solicit input from colleagues across campus for a holistic approach to this student profile.

Above all, keep in mind that bridging the gap using the strategies above is only the first step. True professional development falls within the purview of a counselor's employer, but in a similar spirit, training should be offered routinely to bring new faces up to speed and reinforce agent familiarity with your institution. After all, training is not a one-off item on your agent management checklist, but an essential part of nurturing a strong and productive relationship.

"Partner" Is a Verb

Agents need support to succeed. Support in the application process entails reasonable response times, timely and detailed responses to inquiries, and proactive communication about any changes or updates in programs, admission requirements, deadlines, and scholarships, to name a few.

Partner actively with your agent representatives. Take a hard look at the mechanisms that are in place to support your far-flung teammates, considering especially:

- How and how often do you communicate with them?
- What sort of information are you sharing with them? What information can be shared strategically and what must remain truly internal to institutional employees? Why?

- Is your process responsive to counselor feedback? Is there an opportunity for counselors to give feedback at all? When?
- Are key graduate departments acquainted with your top agents? Do they understand the key role agents play in supporting the enrollment in their programs? Are they prepared to field questions from counselors abroad, or are these inquiries funneled through a central point of contact? A frank assessment of your campus culture and personalities can go a long way to ensuring smooth day-to-day interaction and avoid frustration.

Recognize and Reinforce Success

With each successive intake, more information will become available about the results of your partnership with a given agent. Your due diligence in analyzing the data here can really pay off—especially in the case of larger, multimarket agencies. Concentrations of rejected applications can lend direction and purpose to follow-up training. Are there particular offices or individual counselors who are filing successful applications and driving your yield? How do you, as an institution, reward these counselors for a job well done without running afoul of ethics concerns? A thank you letter, certificate of recognition, feature in an agent newsletter, or other similar no- or low-cost gesture can go a long way toward motivating top-performing agents and impact their peers. Get creative in exploring proactive outreach to boost counselor morale.

Reputable third-party agencies are professional, ethical, and vitally important to supporting both recruitment and admissions activity. Above all, agents want to feel supported by their on-campus partners, accepted as part of the team, and appreciated for their efforts. In a true team-oriented international admissions paradigm, information flows freely and swiftly between institutions and their agent network, training occurs early and often, and success is recognized. The result? A healthy partnership that enshrines a streamlined, consistent, positive student experience at its heart.

References

Bridge Education Group Inc. 2016. *Pace of Adoption of International Student Recruitment Agencies by U.S. Institutions: Market Research Report.* Denver, CO: Bridge Education Group Inc. https://www.bridge.edu/assets/bridge-edu.pdf.

Robert Coelen, "Using Education Agents," European Association for International Education (EAIE) blog, June 30, 2015. http://www.eaie.org/blog/using-education-agents/.

8 PART C

Overseas Representative Offices

By Grant Chapman

While many universities utilize third-party recruiters (e.g., agents) to assist them with international recruitment and admissions, some universities have taken steps to establish their own representative offices within target markets. These representative offices can take many shapes and forms and are established for a variety of reasons. In each case, however, decisionmakers must fully understand and commit to the costs, liabilities, and rewards prior to establishing a physical and legal presence abroad.

The idea of utilizing offshore operations is not new. Many international or multinational companies establish foreign representative offices as a means of mitigating risks or maximizing benefits when branching out across borders. The offices are used to sell the services or goods of a company, source goods, services and capital, and acquire intelligence on the local business cultures, customs, laws, and other issues essential to successfully navigating an international business environment.

While many U.S. universities look to third parties, such as EducationUSA and recruitment agencies, to provide them with an enduring presence abroad, an increasing number are investing in representative offices located within countries designated as having strategic importance for recruitment, research, or other areas.

An international representative office is defined here as a physical and staffed office space located outside of the home country of the sponsoring college or university. While one can argue the difference between an international office and an international representative office, most of the variance is due to legal interpretations and definitions of the word "representative," which can vary from country to country. For instance, the legal requirements of the host country may require the entity to be registered as a "representative" office. This especially tends to be so in cases where the institution contracts with a local entity to carry out the functions of that office.

While it is difficult to find a definitive list of U.S. universities with offices outside the United States, it is not a stretch to say that this is a trend on the rise. The focus of this chapter is on international representative offices established to support the international enrollment strategy of the sponsoring university; however, it is important to note that such entities also may be created for other reasons, such as engaging with international alumni and donors, facilitating study abroad programs, and supporting international research.

What Purpose Is Served by an International Representative Office?

Most, if not all, universities that establish international representative offices do so as part of a larger international outreach strategy. These offices enable institutions to expand engagement beyond the typical few days or weeks spent each year in a target market. As indicated in the table that follows, this year-round presence in the country has benefits for both recruitment and admissions support services.

Table 1: Tasks Related to International Representative Offices

Recruitment Support Services	Admissions Support Services
Interact with agencies, EducationUSA, government officials, and school administrators	Assist applicants to complete applications
Participate in local recruitment activities	Collect admissions materials
Coordinate alumni events	Contact applicants regarding missing materials
Promote academic programs	Evaluate foreign credentials
Gather market intelligence	Interview applicants
Develop promotional materials	Coordinate predeparture orientation

While the purpose for establishing an international representative office will vary from institution to institution, such a major decision requires input and support from multiple stakeholders. This will typically require indisputable evidence of how the office would support the university's mission, vision, and strategic plan.

Webster University set up branch campuses under a transnational education model and was one of the first to develop international branch campuses starting in 1978.

Kansas State University set up an international office to assist with recruiting students from China to the United States and was one of the first to set up such an office in 2006.

Initial Steps

There are many paths to opening an international representative office and the direction taken is often dependent upon the state laws and board policies under which the sponsoring college or university operates, the country in which the office will be registered, and the activities in which the office staff will engage. While it is beyond the scope of this chapter to explore all potential variables, what follows is a simple review process presented as a generic framework for uncovering the variables that are most applicable to a given institution.

Review Cycle for Establishing an International Representative Office

STEP ONE: ESTABLISH RATIONALE

The first step in the review cycle is to establish a clear rationale for opening the international representative office. It is important to fully consider and clearly articulate the strategic goals and challenges that would be addressed by an international representative office since establishing such an entity represents a major investment on the part of the sponsoring institution.

FIGURE 1

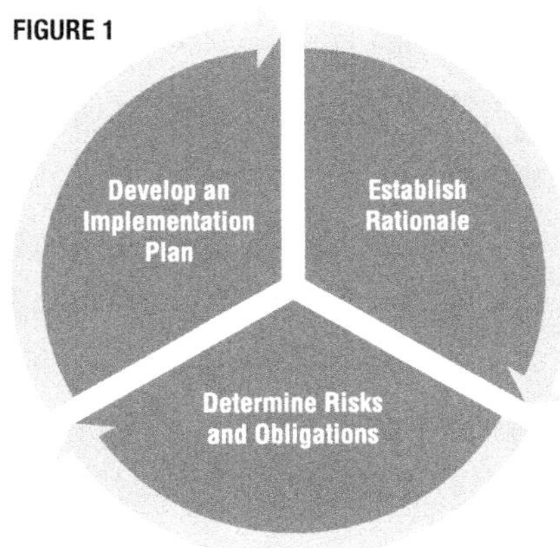

The rationale will vary from institution to institution. In some instances, it will be because of historical ties to a particular country. In other cases, the primary driver will be to expand capacity for the recruitment of students and promotion of future academic collaborations. The office may also serve as an alternative to contracting with agents in a specific market or it may be part of an institution's agency-based recruitment strategy and serve as a local resource for agency partners. Regardless of the purpose, it is very important that the motive be clearly understood and supported by key decisionmakers.

STEP TWO: DETERMINE RISKS AND OBLIGATIONS

The second step is to determine not only the financial, legal and reputational risks associated with establishing an international representative office, but also to meticulously document the obligations that come with establishing a legal presence overseas. The term "global operations" is increasingly used to refer to the administrative, financial, and legal considerations associated with conducting the business of higher education outside of one's own country. Several universities and higher education systems (see University of California Global Operations) now have websites and teams devoted to global operations.

While procedures, policies, and resources related to global operations are still underdeveloped at many institutions, the discussions that take place with key internal (e.g., staff from budget, human resources, and legal counsel) and external (e.g., outside counsel with expertise in global operations, U.S. and foreign government officials, and administrators from other institutions who have experience in successfully establishing an international representative office in the target country) stakeholders as a result of the fact-finding activities in step two will inevitably push the topic to the surface.

Useful Websites

University of California Global Operations
http://www.ucgo.org/

University of Washington
https://f2.washington.edu/fm/globalsupport/home

University of Minnesota
https://global.umn.edu/operations/#/0

Columbia University
http://finance.columbia.edu/departments/global-support

STEP THREE: DEVELOP AN IMPLEMENTATION PLAN

The final step in the review cycle is the development of an implementation plan. This should incorporate feedback gathered during the previous two stages and include the following components:

- Project Charter or Purpose of Entity that clearly and succinctly defines the strategic objectives, stakeholders and executive champion(s);
- Work plan that displays phases, milestones, and prerequisite tasks (i.e., tasks ordered by dependencies) along an agreed upon timeline;
- Identification of potential risks and strategies for mitigating them;
- Approved budget with identified funding sources;
- Change management process for reducing conflict and scope creep; and
- Agreement(s)/contract(s) that outline key terms such as use of trademarks and logos, authorized exports and imports, licenses, and safeguards to ensure the university maintains control of academic decisions.

It also helps to develop customized checklists related to the various tasks required by this project.

A due diligence checklist can be modified depending on the specifications of the proposed international representative office (see Resource 1).

As Figure 1 on page 97 indicates, the review process is an ongoing cycle that requires continuous assessment. To ensure the international representative office remains relevant, responsible parties should regularly review its purpose and charge and make modifications to meet the evolving needs of the university, changes to local regulations, or market demand.

Resource 1

An International Representative Office Consideration Checklist

1) **Home campus, home country considerations:**

   a. Who ultimately approves the international office?

      i. President and/or Provost (or Chief Academic Officer)
      ii. Board of Regents or Board of Trustees
      iii. Other university unit—Chief Financial or Administrative Officer
      iv. Other governmental unit—governor's office, local State Department of Education

   b. Who should be involved when starting an international office? (depends on purpose and scope of office)

      i. The above in 1) a.
      ii. Legal counsel (or outside counsel)
      iii. Finance and Administration Units
      iv. Risk Management Unit
      v. International Programs Unit
      vi. Enrollment Management Unit
      vii. Research and Collaboration
      viii. Particular academic units—schools, colleges, centers, and institutes
      ix. Alumni Affairs
      x. Outreach and/or Extension
      xi. Development (Foundation)
      xii. Other

   c. What specific regulations, rules, and policies would govern the international office?

      i. Federal regulations (in areas such as sanctions, export controls, licensing, etc.)
      ii. State regulations
      iii. Regulations of the host country
      iv. University's charter or statute
      v. Trustees, regents, governing boards
      vi. University handbook, policies and procedures
      vii. Legal, finance, and administration policies and procedures
      viii. Other

   d. To which unit does the international office report?

      i. International Programs
      ii. Outreach and Extension
      iii. The President's Office
      iv. The Provost's (Chief Academic Officer's) Office
      v. Enrollment Management Unit
      vi. Research and Collaboration Unit
      vii. Alumni Affairs and/or Development
      viii. A particular academic unit
      ix. Other

(continued)

Resource 1: An International Representative Office Consideration Checklist (continued)

2) **Host country considerations:**
   a. Are there country-specific risks?—understand the political and economic risks.
   b. What are the legal requirements?—federal, regional, and local requirements in setting up an entity forming an international office.
   c. What types of business entities can be formed?—understand what types of business entities are allowable.
   d. What are the financial and investment requirements?—understand requirements concerning investment, repatriation, and audit of an international office.
   e. Are there particular cultural business norms?—understand the culture of having a local entity as an international office of a foreign higher educational institution.
   f. Who can best identify appropriate individuals to represent the university and understand the local culture?—find and train the type of individual to accurately and effective represent the university or college culture while understanding the local culture.
   g. Use local resources from embassies, EducationUSA, Institute of International Education (IIE) offices, and Fulbright commissions to form a country profile.
   h. Solicit advice from alumni who have business, legal, or other relevant expertise within the host country.
   i. What partnerships are required to ensure adequate administrative oversight? Consider local accountants and attorneys for routine financial and legal audits.
   j. Would staff in the host country be expected to travel to areas to which the home country staff would generally be prohibited from visiting due to health and safety concerns?
   k. Are there similar representative offices already in the target market? Do they represent competitors?
   l. What is the exit plan for closing down operations in the host country? Will staff and equipment need to be repatriated?

Supporting the Newly Established International Representative Office

Input from all offices, understanding one's own institution's governance system, and advice and due diligence by legal counsel and the finance and administration staff are important. However, the most important piece in this complicated puzzle is the relationship between the international representative office and the university. There needs to be constant communications and training that is open, bilateral, and informative. In addition, staff based at the international representative office should have access to necessary information, such as the status of specific applications, and systems (see chapter 8, part F for a discussion on how international representative office staff can increase the efficiency of admission workflows). In the end, there is no substitute for the international representative office staff to feel that they are an integral part of the sponsoring college or university.

Conclusion

International representative offices have several functions including recruitment, alumni activities, managing partnership or collaborative programs, managing exchanges, managing research, and serving as a resource for in-country faculty, staff, and student travel. These entities represent major investments, but also genuine commitments to international engagement. The keys to their success are clarifying the strategic objectives they will support and supporting them as true extensions of the university.

8 PART D

International Admissions: Financing Higher Education

By Blair Brown

A growing number of higher education institutions around the world have aggressively pursued increases in international student enrollment over the past decade. The Institute of International Education's (IIE) 2016 *Open Doors* report indicates that there are 1,043,839 international students enrolled in the United States (IIE 2016). In spite of this record enrollment, the financing of higher education for international students coming to the United States remains much more nuanced than financing for domestic students, and several factors contribute to the financial stability of international students at both a macro and micro level.

Restrictions on Eligibility for Institutional Aid

Institutional scholarships tend to be more limited for international students. One reason for this is that the eligibility requirements for merit-based awards are often based upon class rank, ACT scores, or SAT scores, which may immediately disqualify international students whose schools do not publish a class rank or for whom it is impossible (e.g., no local testing center) or impractical (e.g., the student requires intensive English instruction) to take the ACT or SAT. It is also the case that an international student's grade point average (GPA), which may not be weighted, is often compared to U.S. high school GPAs, which increasingly are weighted. For these and other policy or procedural reasons, international students may be disadvantaged or entirely excluded from considerations for merit-based funding. At some institutions, this phenomenon is also true at the graduate level, particularly in programs housed in departments that are not research intensive.

Of course, there are also less concrete reasons why institutional aid may be limited for international students. First, at public institutions, giving away scholarship funds to nonresident students, regardless of whether or not they are international, may be negatively perceived by taxpayers, legislators, and other stakeholders. This is especially true as Americans continue to pay higher costs to finance their education, and, consequentially, take on higher debt (Bird and Turner 2014). Second, international students must show financial solvency in order to receive their respective visa document and so it may be assumed that there is no need for further financing after initial funds are verified by school officials. Third, international students are increasingly viewed as a source of tuition revenue and such a perspective often precludes the notion that international students may be price sensitive or require assistance in overcoming financial difficulties.

Restrictions on Eligibility for Federal, State, and Private Aid

Another challenge is that information on institutional websites, brochures, and other public documents intended for domestic applicants may lead some international applicants to mistakenly believe they are eligible for financial aid from the U.S. government. This may lead them to attempt to complete a Free Application for Federal Student Aid (FAFSA) even when they are typically not eligible for loans or awards from the U.S. federal government.

There are also restrictions at the state level, but these vary from state to state. In some instances, international students will not be eligible for any form of aid while in others they may receive a loan only if a U.S. citizen or legal permanent resident is listed as a cosigner. Similarly, some states may permit international students to be classified as residents for tuition purposes while others may explicitly prohibit this practice.

Private loans can be an option for international students, but many U.S. financial lenders require Social Security numbers, a credit history, or a cosigner who is a U.S. citizen or legal permanent resident in order for a loan application to be considered. Most international students are unable to satisfy these requirements.

Regardless of whether the source of aid is federal, state, or private, the fact remains that there is a definite knowledge gap with regards to funding options available to international applicants. One thing international admissions professionals can do to remedy this problem is to ensure that all information about financial aid produced and distributed by the institution includes language clarifying who is the intended audience. This may also include the development of special webpages, brochures, and scholarship listings for international students.

Currency Exchange Rates and Economic Downturns

The recent strength of the U.S. dollar has, in relative terms, made an education in the United States vastly more expensive for new and continuing students alike. Fluctuations in currency exchange rates can result in students paying a significant amount more in their local currency even when the tuition remains flat in terms of U.S. dollars. When foreign currencies lose value against the dollar, it results in enormous barriers to entry and retention of international students from those affected countries. This can lead to financial instability and uncertainty that is unsustainable. The result is that students may feel obligated to continue their education in countries with currency that is "weaker" than the U.S. dollar, transfer to other U.S. institutions where scholarships may be more abundant, or simply return home without having completed their educational objectives.

Helping International Students Finance Higher Education

Campus leaders should take this issue of financing international students seriously. Often, international recruitment and admissions professionals are tasked with quickly increasing the number of international students, but this can have a deleterious effect on the institution's reputation and the experiences of students when not done in a strategic, integrated manner.

Campus leaders should commit to a comprehensive plan for supporting international student enrollment that is based on goals beyond simply increasing the institution's bottom line. Such an approach requires stakeholders to consider the academic, cultural, and other benefits provided by the presence of international students.

Three specific strategies for helping international students finance higher education include:

- **Emergency Fund:** A portion of the revenue generated from international student enrollment may be redirected to an emergency fund from which funds may be provided to worthy students in the form of a loan or grant. It is generally a good idea to establish an application process by which students may request funding, criteria (e.g., 3.0 or higher GPA and final semester before graduation) for reviewing requests, and a committee to assist in determining award amounts. If members of the committee are from other units, such as financial aid or the student's college, then it may be possible to stack awards from multiple sources so as to craft a solid financial package without maxing out the emergency fund.
- **Tuition Discount:** Such initiatives typically keep the tuition amount set at a rate that is higher than the cost of education, but low enough so that the student may afford to enroll. These are generally strategic decisions made in an effort to attract talented students, increase diversity of nationalities represented on campus, or achieve other institutional objectives.
- **Tuition Install Plan:** Such programs, where available, are typically accessible to all students and allow tuition to be paid over a set number of installments throughout the semester. In many instances, institutions assess a nominal fee for enrolling in such a program.

In closing, it is important for international educators to help other faculty and staff recognize the challenges international students face in financing their education. While some of the actions that can be taken to assist students require an investment on the part of the institution, others simply represent a shift in practice. Institutions are generally prepared to ride high on the waves of economic prosperity when times are good, but they should equally be committed to supporting students in need when times are tough.

References

Bird, Kelli, and Sarah Turner. "College in the States: Foreign Student Demand and Higher Education Supply in the U.S." *EdPolicyWorks* Working Paper Series No. 23. April 2014. Available at http://curry.virginia.edu/uploads/resourceLibrary/23_Bird_Foreign_Student_Demand.pdf.

Institute of International Education. 2016. *Open Doors Report on International Educational Exchange*. Retrieved from http://www.iie.org/en/Research-and-Publications/Open-Doors/Data/International-Students#.WJTG-mQrKAy.

8 PART E

The Nuts and Bolts of International Admissions Operations

By Jon Weller

There are many regulations that guide the student visa and immigration processes of international students. However, there are far fewer regulations guiding the implementation of international admissions procedures. This section addresses many of the practical, nuts and bolts issues of managing admissions operations related to international students.

Note that this section will focus only on degree-seeking international students and not exchange students, visiting students, or students studying in intensive English programs—though many of the issues outlined here may be relevant to these groups as well.

Defining International Students

As discussed in chapter 2, defining "international students" can be complicated, and setting policies and rules for "international students" can be difficult given the tremendous diversity of students and educational systems throughout the world. Distinguishing between domestic and international students is important because some institutions may have separate applications, documentation requirements, application deadlines, and application readers depending on whether a student is considered domestic or international.

International Students at Foreign Institutions

Most international students are individuals who were born outside the United States, have studied at foreign institutions, and must follow the U.S. Department of State visa regulations and the U.S. Department of Homeland

Security's immigration regulations in order to be eligible to enter the United States to begin their studies.

International Students in U.S. Institutions

While many international applicants are located outside the United States, universities can also successfully enroll international students who are currently studying within the United States. These students have much to offer a university—including the unique perspective of being an international student with a deeper understanding of American language and culture. However, defining the enrollment processes that they follow can be complicated. For example, should a student who has been living and studying in the United States for 5 years be required to follow the same admissions procedures as her American classmates? Should a high school exchange student who arrives in August of his senior year be required to submit SAT/ACT scores by an institution's fall application deadline? Should a student who has been in the United States for over a year, but has been taking ESL courses rather than English courses, be exempt from submitting TOEFL or IELTS scores? Should such students be admitted by the domestic admissions office or the international admissions office?

U.S. Citizens in Foreign Institutions

Just as there are international students studying in U.S. higher education institutions, there are also U.S. citizens/permanent residents studying in foreign institutions. These students can also bring unique perspectives to campus based on their experiences of being a U.S. citizen who has lived for an extended period of time outside the United States. However, their enrollment processes can also be more complicated. For example, should a U.S. citizen who was born in the United States but moved home to China when he or she was a toddler be required to follow the procedures for international applicants or domestic applicants? Should a U.S. citizen who has only studied in the traditional Indian education system be expected to follow the admissions deadlines of domestic students or international students?

A possible way to clarify the appropriate enrollment procedures for such students is to look not only at their citizenship status, but also at the length of time that they have been studying at the particular institution. For example, a university may decide that a U.S. student who will have completed more than 2 years of high school study in the United States by the time he or she graduates should follow the procedures for domestic students, whereas an international student who has completed fewer than 2 years of study in the United States should follow the procedures of traditional international students.

Differences Between Graduate and Undergraduate Admissions

It is important to note that there are many common differences between undergraduate and graduate admissions processes. Undergraduate admissions processes are often centralized where institutional faculty set admissions requirements, or guidelines, but the admissions decisions are made by university administrators. The application process is often standardized with clear admissions deadlines, notification timelines, and a concentrated effort on customer service.

By contrast, graduate admission processes are often decentralized. There is often a central graduate admissions office that promotes graduate programs and collects application materials; however, the materials are often forwarded to graduate faculty committees for file review. It is common that different graduate programs at the same university will have different application and notification deadlines, as well as different levels of customer services (such as responsiveness to student inquiries).

In both cases, however, undergraduate and graduate admissions processes require students to submit predetermined documentation, such as standardized test scores, writing samples, and transcripts, and adhere to posted deadlines.

Admissions Documentation Requirements

Unofficial or Official Transcripts?

International students often have unique challenges in submitting high school and/or university transcripts, which may include expensive shipping costs and difficulty in receiving multiple (if any) sets of official transcripts. This has resulted in some institutions adopting modified document requirements, such as only accepting copies of transcripts that are certified or attested by a local EducationUSA office or allowing international students to scan transcripts rather than mail them. However, recently technical changes have also impacted the document submission process. The Common Application, for example, allows domestic and international undergraduate students to upload transcripts directly from their high schools, thereby eliminating the need to mail the documents. Similarly, many graduate admissions offices are now allowing students to submit scanned copies of transcripts with the requirement that they submit a final, official set of transcripts if they are admitted. Notably, several graduate admission offices are requiring transcripts from Chinese universities to be vetted through the China Academic Degrees and Graduate Education Development Center (CDGDC) after a student is admitted but before the student is allowed to accept his or her offer of admission.

Credential Evaluation Requirements

Degree programs will obviously require students to submit transcripts. However, there are distinct differences in how the transcripts are evaluated once they are received. Some institutions have in-house credential evaluators who are trusted to review international high school and/or university transcripts and determine their authenticity. These in-house evaluators may also recommend, or determine, the amount of transfer credit the student may receive. Conversely, other universities essentially outsource the credential evaluation process to third-party organizations. These institutions may require that students work with one particular vendor, or work with any member of the National Association of Credential Evaluation Services (NACES), or allow students to select any vendor of their choice. Outsourcing this process to third-party vendors limits institutional liability of admitting students based on fraudulent documentation. However, from the student's perspective, it can also further complicate the admissions process and increase the application cost, resulting in students not applying to institutions that require such processes.

Standardized Test Score Requirements

ACADEMIC TEST SCORE REQUIREMENTS

International graduate applicants are generally required to submit the same standardized test scores (GRE, MBA, etc.) as their U.S. counterparts. However, there tends to be more diversion at the undergraduate level. Some institutions require international students to follow the same standardized test score requirements as U.S. students. Others provide greater flexibility for international students, who live in countries where opportunities to take the SAT and/or ACT can be extremely limited and requiring students to take such standardized tests could force them to travel to different cities, or even countries, simply to take a test. Regardless of the policy, universities need to post the policy publically and enforce it consistently to ensure all applicants are following the same guidelines.

ENGLISH LANGUAGE REQUIREMENTS

The U.S. Department of Homeland Security provides detailed regulations regarding the Form I-20 or Form DS-2019 issuance process of universities. Among these is Section 214.3(K), which requires institutions to certify that a student has met all admissions standards, including English proficiency requirements, prior to the issuance of a Form I-20 or Form DS-2019. As we shall see, these English proficiency requirements may include both standardized test scores, such as TOEFL or IELTS, or alternative methods, such as having studied in an English-speaking country. These requirements can be quite complicated and vary significantly between, and even within, undergraduate and graduate programs. For example, a highly competitive undergraduate program that requires excellent communication skills may have higher language requirements than a graduate program at the same institution. Conversely, an undergraduate program may have lower English language requirements because students will be on campus for a longer period of time and the institution is able to provide the necessary language and cultural support to the student throughout their studies.

Some institutions not only require minimum overall test scores but also require minimum scores on each subscore of the standardized test. The primary intent of this method is to ensure students have adequate skills across all aspects of English communication. For example, a student with an overall Internet-based TOEFL (iBT) score of 82 but with a score of 12 on the speaking section may not be accepted, while a student with an overall score of 79 but no subscore below 15 is accepted.

EXEMPTIONS TO ENGLISH STANDARDIZED TEST SCORE

Although standardized language scores, such as TOEFL and IELTS, are common for international applicants, there can be many ways to exempt students from such requirements. Perhaps the most common exemption for English proficiency test scores is for students who have studied in English-speaking countries and/or institutions. Though certain examples may be fairly obvious—a student who graduated from the London School of Economics, for example—institutions may vary on which countries they feel are truly (even if officially) English speaking. Additionally, institutions may have different requirements for evidence that English is taught appropriately at institutions located in non-English-speaking countries. Whereas some universities may issue blanket exemptions based on the language of instruction, others may have more narrowed requirements, such as students having to have earned certain grades in certain courses at the institution or requiring the students to participate in an interview before an exemption to a standardized test is provided.

International Admissions Stakeholders

This section has addressed several of the major practical nuts and bolts components of the international admissions process. Bearing in mind that U.S. higher education institutions are known for their uniqueness, it is not possible to recommend one-size-fits-all solutions to the issues outlined above. However, given that international students usually make up a relatively small proportion of a U.S. institution's overall student population (particularly in regards to undergraduate students) and that "international students" do not follow a universal path leading to an institution's front door, it is important for institutions to identify campus stakeholders, or decisionmakers, to address the specific needs and areas of enrollment management ambiguity that can face international applicants.

Academic Requirements

As mentioned previously, faculty are often empowered to set the academic criteria of their programs. This is often a responsibility that faculty hold in high value. However, particularly in regards to international undergraduate enrollment efforts, faculty may not be familiar with the academic credentials, or market practices, of the international student recruitment industry in general, or in particular regions and/or countries. Therefore, identifying a special team of faculty members and administrators with international enrollment expertise that can review academic credentials and establish appropriate academic requirements will help avoid confusing application processes for international applicants—and international admission offices. The overall intent of this group should be to ensure that the academic credentials established are not only helping the institution meet its enrollment goals, but also ensuring that the international students are likely to succeed when they arrive on campus.

Document Requirements

Academic documentation requirements of a particular institution may be set by administrators, faculty, or even a Board of Trustees. Those setting such requirements may not be as familiar with the nuances of international documentation issues, but a designated group can help establish the necessary guidelines in this scenario as well. Such a group will want to balance the documentation needs to evaluate application materials with the desire to open or restrict access for international students. For example, one institution hoping to aggressively grow international enrollment may create a simplified admissions process, which may eliminate the application fee and allow for scanned copies of transcripts, while an institution more focused on quality and "fit" of students may have more regimented admissions documentation procedures, such as not providing application fee waivers and requiring essays.

Conclusion

As evidenced by this chapter, many considerations must be made in order to properly address the nuts and bolts of international admissions. While actual practices will vary from institution to institution, it is imperative that international admissions not occur within a vacuum or be relegated to the sidelines of administrative decisionmaking. Failure to accomplish these basic objectives will result in policy, procedural, and other major changes being implemented without proper consideration of their impact on international applicants.

A successful international admissions unit requires understanding, support, and input from a wide range of campus constituents. This can only be achieved by engaging stakeholders based outside of the international admissions office. At some institutions it may be most appropriate to discuss the international dimensions of admissions with a university-wide admissions or enrollment management committee. At other institutions, it may make more sense to establish a stand-alone group focused exclusively on issues pertaining to international admissions. In either instance, this collaborative approach will help educate key faculty, staff, and administrators about international admissions while at the same time soliciting valuable insights from technical experts and decisionmakers alike.

8 PART F

International-Friendly Application Process

By Ted R. McKown, II

Efficiency when processing applications is a key to effective international recruitment. Applicants who receive quick admission decisions and Forms I-20 or DS-2019 apply for visas to secure the dream of studying in the United States. Processing application and immigration documents quickly and efficiently should be a high priority for an international admissions office. An electronic application process that is expeditious can positively impact the enrollment process. Winning the race to get a complete acceptance packet to the student first is important to eventually enrolling the student on your campus.

There are three factors that directly influence the applicant's decision to enroll when applying to an institution: the amount of time it takes to process an individual's application, the connection that is established with the university during the admissions process, and the cost of attendance. The latter can be controlled and manipulated through discounting and scholarships, but there is not a direct correlation to the application process. A connection to the university is enhanced after the applicant applies, but begins very early during the admissions cycle. While there are many ways to implement efficiencies throughout the admissions process, an electronic process can add the greatest speed. The time it takes your office to process an application may be the concluding factor in whether or not an international student enrolls on your campus.

International admissions can be broken down into many elements: marketing and recruitment, application requirements and processing, admissions decisions, as well as processing Forms I-20 or DS-2019 at many institutions. Admissions professionals may be sound in their recruitment efforts, effective at processing applications, and conduct admissions procedures to the highest ethical standards, but these skills, tools, and practices do not guarantee success in enrolling students. Students must feel engaged within the application process at all times to keep an institution on the top of their mind. Consistent and timely communications are not always the strong suit of the U.S. university (Cynamon Mayers 2014). An electronic application workflow is an effective way to draw the international student to your college or university in an expeditious manner.

Charles Nieman, director of international affairs at Shepherd University, conducted international student satisfaction surveys at a large university in the U.S. Midwest. As a part of the research, Nieman (1998) reviewed the overall satisfaction of international students with the admissions process. He found that international students needed three elements from the admissions process to commit to the institution: speed of application process, appropriate pricing point and financial structure including financial aid, and a relational connection to the institution.

Nearly two decades later these insights remain relevant as the 2016 Agent Barometer demonstrates that the most important concern for recruitment agents is "quick response time to enquiries and application and regular communication updates." Yet, while efficient process of international admissions seems to be a basic concern for many, a 2014 mystery shopper experiment conducted by Intead not only found significant delays on the part of institutions responding to inquiries from an international applicant, but that 23 (21 percent) of the 80 institutions targeted in this experiment never responded at all. In other writings, McKown (2009) discusses engaging the international student adviser in the admissions process. This is an attempt to add high-touch marketing into the mix and connect the international student to the university through relationships.

Before you communicate with prospective international students, it is important to know the student's preferred conduit of communication. If an applicant prefers to receive text messages when your office sends letters through the mail, you will not communicate your message to the customer. Your letter will not be read by the person to whom it is intended. Many international students prefer text messages, social media, and e-mail today. Recent surveys of college-bound students revealed that mail and e-mail are not dead. Rather, they are a preferred and trusted form of college search and application communication for the applicant. Therefore, mailings and e-mail are still a critical form of an admissions communication plan today in spite of college-bound students' preferences to use modern technology and social media (Rogers and Sickler 2016). A communications mix that includes all of these elements is ideal.

However, it may not be feasible for your office or institution to incorporate all elements. Strategic decisions must be made based on your institutional situation and your target market as to which platforms you will use. Regardless of your decision, you can optimize your communications plan by simply using a customer relationship management (CRM) tool to manage it. Customer relationship management is a platform that allows marketers to facilitate customer interactions and take advantage of trends within historical analysis to increase application activity and yield to enrollment. A CRM tool allows international admissions representatives to manage relationships with prospective students much like a brand manager would maintain the product market share. Institutions that use a CRM tool may generate more qualified leads and applications as well as improve yield with admits and enrolled students.

The most important factor in choosing an institution of higher learning in the United States for an international student may be the speed at which you process their application and how effectively you communicate throughout the process. Electronic systems allow the admissions professional to manage a high volume of application activity while not compromising a personalized process. Electronic systems that should be a part of the admissions process begin with a clear and concise online application, a workflow system to process the application electronically, and electronic communications throughout the entire process from initial application communications to notification on the delivery of Forms I-20 or DS-2019.

A realistic process time for an undergraduate international application to an institution within the United States utilizing electronic processes is 72–120 hours. This would mean that any undergraduate application should take no longer than one business week to process. Satisfying this type of process window would require utilization of quick and efficient document analysis, as well as a workflow system to expedite decisionmaking. The end result in the admissions process is enrollment, which means this process does not end with the application. Immigration document issuance must be included within this timeframe. While other elements of the application can be processed electronically, Forms I-20 or DS-2019 must be mailed. It is recommended to mail the Forms I-20 or DS-2019 via an express mail courier.

The next section discusses three electronic methods for improving the admissions process: the electronic application, a customer relationship management system that will manage all communications, and an electronic workflow system to process applications.

Electronic Application

Electronic applications have become common in the field of admissions in the United States. These web-based forms can be homegrown or commercially available enterprise solutions. Whether you develop your application or pay an outside vendor to create it, it is very helpful to utilize a system through which the application can automatically download or share information with your institution's student information system. This allows for congruence in interacting from qualified lead to applicant so that you can strengthen the relational bond with the future student.

Customer Relationship Management (CRM) System

Developing a system to manage customer relationships at lightning speed is a key to effectively getting international students to your campus. Building relationships requires your office to efficiently send a multitude of communications. Automated messages set up with a CRM tool can keep the communication pipeline flowing, keeping the qualified lead well informed. Some CRMs have the ability to handle the development of an online application.

This method allows stored lead data to instantly download at the time the applicant submits the application.

While a CRM tool can make it easier to communicate with prospects and applicants, it is important to not overcommunicate by bombarding individuals with information they don't find valuable. Try to communicate with at least one relevant message per week that is personalized and automated. This allows the prospective student to receive the needed information and keeps your institution on the top of the student's mind. An automated approach is front-loaded with setup but pays major dividends in the end.

Electronic Workflow

Once application materials are received and the application is complete, the admission review can begin. While some admissions decisions may be as easy as a computer algorithm set with established parameters, others may have to go through departmental or collegial committees where many people need to review the same application in order to make a decision. It is possible this wide procedural spectrum exists at the same institution. Due to this supposition, an electronic workflow of application materials can allow multiple users to review application materials simultaneously, track the status of each decisionmaker, and provide time limits for delinquent reviewers.

The application review process can be complicated at a U.S. college or university. Multiple decisionmakers within the review timeframe can bog down the tight window of application completion. While it is helpful to limit the amount of hands that touch an application, it is not necessary to do so if you can use technology to process the application. An electronic workflow allows scanned and indexed application materials to move digitally from one reviewer to the next and even facilitate simultaneous assessment. It is important to begin with a goal when establishing the electronic process. This will allow decisionmakers to get on the same page and work toward the common goals of international student enrollment and maintain a mandated quality control on the electronic application process.

Personalizing the application process can be critical as well. Continuing the automated communication plan through a time of application is the first step. Applicants need to feel comfortable as they apply to your institution. Providing the application in another language can help with the comfort level in completing the form and providing accurate information. This can provide the connection an applicant needs to commit as a student to your institution.

Be wary of waiving or deferring application fees. Fee waivers or deferment leads to ghost applications or applicants who submit an application to your institution who may not be the best fit for your school or may never have true intentions to enroll. There are ways to allow the applicant to pay the application fee in their local currency. However, this sometimes can be costly to the university. An institution may decide to pay for or refund the student for currency exchange or wire transfer fees. The institution must decide at what cost it is willing to have international students and how many on campus. Your institution may also decide to contract with a third-party agency or wire transfer service to collect this fee. At a minimum, the college or university can provide a foreign currency quote for the applicant.

In-country support staff can provide a conduit between the applicant and the admissions office. Such representatives may be regular employees temporarily or permanently stationed abroad, independent contractors, alumni, or even agents whom the institution has authorized to collect and submit admissions materials. The materials may include the application itself, application fee, and any other documentation needed for the application such as transcripts, proof of English language proficiency, letters of recommendation, essays, portfolios, and financial documentation. The in-country support staff can collect all materials or just certain elements of the application that meet your comfort level, but it is critical that the individuals to whom this responsibility is delegated are appropriately trained about the institution's admissions policies, procedures and document submission processes. Additionally, the international admissions office should employ a nearly paperless process so as to limit costs and delays associated with mailing. In-country support staff could utilize technology such as a file transfer protocol (FTP), virtual private network (VPN) or even cloud-based applications so long as they satisfy the security standards of the institution.

Initial academic records can be sent by satellite senders if properly trained to collect appropriate documentation. Satellite senders can verify true originals and e-mail copies of the documents. A collection of materials can happen as quickly as 24 hours from the time of application with this type of system.

The best action step an admissions representative can take to improve the international enrollment is to convert to an electronic application process that narrows the timeframe between initial application and Form I-20 or Form DS-2019 issuance. Processing and issuing Forms I-20 or DS-2019 is just as important to the admissions process as processing the application itself. As stated, speed of application process, which should include Forms I-20 or DS-2019 issuance, wins the international student enrollment game.

An argument in higher education might be related to how much an international student should pay for the cost of education. Regardless of philosophical issues or institutional policy and procedure, an international student will only pay the amount that they are willing and able to pay. Therefore, the tuition pricing point must be set appropriately as well as other expenses and fees. The pricing point should be adjusted with scholarships or discounts if international enrollment is truly a priority at your institution.

The ability to manage relationships within a multilayered system requires a good relationship management system and quality admissions personnel committed to bridging a relational gap between the institution and potential student. Step one is to build a communication plan from the initial contact to enrollment and then automate the plan into a CRM tool. Within the plan should be personal connections made by your staff following up on the applicant's intentions and action to move forward in the process at every step within the admissions funnel. A communications plan should include e-mails, social media, Robo calls, text messages, videos, electronic cards, scripted calls made by admissions professionals that communicate the messages of the institution in terms of admissions, tuition, and financial aid, academic program offerings, student services, as well as cultural dialogue.

As mentioned earlier, international students today communicate through social media, texting, and e-mail. Mobile devices are used to look at institutions' websites, apply, and send messages. Please remember that e-mail and snail mail are not dead when referring to the admissions process. They are still relevant in communicating to today's applicant. Develop your communication plan and processes with this in mind to reach the intended market.

References

Lisa Cynamon Mayers, "The Intead Mystery Shopper Strikes Again! (Part 1)" Recruiting Intelligence (Blog), Intead: International Education Advantage, LLC, December 9, 2014, http://services.intead.com/blog/the-intead-mystery-shopper-strikes-again.

McKown, II, Theodore. 2009. "Synergizing admissions and advising to improve international recruitment." In *International students: Strengthening a critical resource*, ed. M. Andrade and N. Evans. Plymouth: R&L Education.

Nieman, Charles L., "Web-based evaluation of overall international student satisfaction: The case of Kent State University" (dissertation, Kent State University, 1998).

Peppers, Don, and Martha Rogers. 1993. *The One to One Future: Building Relationships One Customer at a Time*. New York: Doubleday.

Rogers, Gil, and Eric Sickler. TeensTalk 2016: Key Influencers at Key Phases of the College Search. Stamats Chegg 2016. Available from http://go.edu.chegg.com/TeensTALK-2016.

8 PART G

Intensive English Programs

By David B. Woodward

Intensive English Program (IEP) admissions practices in the United States have recently undergone and continue to undergo systemic and noteworthy changes since the adoption of the Accreditation of English Language Training Programs Act in December 2010, its implementation on December 13, 2013, and the final SEVP Policy Guidance (S13.1) for Conditional Admission issued on July 13, 2016. These changes to federal law and policy with regard to IEP admissions have been accompanied by dramatic developments in the field of international education. This includes severe funding cuts for government scholarships from oil-producing countries due to the massive drop in oil prices during the 2014–2015 academic year and economic downturns in many leading G-20 economies. IEPs tend to be the proverbial "canary in the coal mine" of international education and as such serve as a leading indicator of global trends for the field as a whole. In this chapter we will briefly review these aforementioned factors as well as summarize the types of IEP program models, partnership models, demographics served, criteria for admissions decisionmaking, essentials of IEP admission processes, and how IEPs can augment academic admissions practices.

Impact of the 2010 ESL Accreditation Act on IEP Admissions

The Accreditation of English Language Training Programs Act passed by Congress in December 2010 was the first of its kind in the history of the IEP field. Its passage instituted an accreditation requirement for IEPs prior to receiving SEVP authorization or maintaining SEVP authorization to issue

Form I-20s (and thereby enrolling foreign students on F-1 and M-1 visas), thereby making accreditation essential to the viability of most if not all IEPs in the United States. Most IEPs in the United States as of January 2011 did not have accreditation specific to ESL operations, although IEPs being operated by universities and colleges typically utilized institutional accreditation to satisfy U.S. Department of Homeland Security requirements.

Between January 2011 and December 13, 2013, all IEPs were required to demonstrate that they had accreditation specific to ESL operations whether it was via regional academic accreditation or national accreditation bodies. The only organizations capable of providing national accreditation to nonacademic third-party providers were the Commission on English Language Program Accreditation (CEA) and the Accrediting Council for Continuing Education and Training (ACCET). As a result, these two accrediting bodies experienced an overwhelming demand for rapid turnaround for hundreds of private IEPs.

Regional accrediting bodies also experienced a surge of requests by universities and colleges for ESL-specific accreditation. In early 2014, the Student and Exchange Visitor Program (SEVP) issued a quarterly report indicating that the number of institutions authorized to issue Form I-20s had declined in the prior quarter, significantly representing the likely closure of several hundred IEPs due to the December 13, 2013 deadline for implementation of the accreditation requirement. From that point forward, the process of starting up, accrediting, and gaining authorization to issue Form I-20s for an IEP changed in fundamental ways. It is beyond the purview of this brief overview to examine the various accreditation options for IEPs in depth, but suffice it to say that there are significant variations in accreditation as there are significant variations in types and models of IEP operations.

Impact of SEVP's Final Determination on Conditional Admission Procedures as It Pertains to IEP Admissions

As with the Accreditation Act, SEVP's Final Policy Guidance (S13.1) for Conditional Admission issued on July 13, 2016, is a key landmark in the topography of IEP development and operations. This policy guidance was heralded in May 2013 when SEVP announced a review of interpretation and practice for DHS immigration regulations including the utilization of conditional admissions by academic institutions to accommodate the needs of foreign students transitioning into a full course of study. Historically, IEPs routinely started up operations or maintained operations by relying on associated academic host institutions issuing Form I-20s on behalf of IEPs rather than applying for SEVP certification and gaining authorization independently. If the prospective student was considered to not have already met the English proficiency requirement of the institution issuing the Form I-20, the nature of the admission was considered "conditional" and typically the Form I-20 would include a notation to this effect.

The Final SEVP Policy Guidance (S13.1) "prohibits the issuance of a Form I-20 based on conditional admission. DSOs can only issue a Form I-20 when students have met all standards for admission for the program of study listed on the Form I-20. These standards for admission include any English proficiency requirements." The impact of this guidance is to disallow the startup or continued operation of an IEP that does not already have SEVP certification. This is a crucial distinction for IEPs that do not already have a student population sufficient to maintain business operations that are required for successful attainment of accreditation and subsequent ESL-specific SEVP certification. This could be referred to as the IEP "Catch 22." This guidance likewise has significant consequences for all "pathway programs" that are conditional in nature. With the popularity of such programs as a way for institutions to rapidly internationalize an institution's demographics, the impact of this guidance on programs without the requisite authorization to issue Form I-20s could be significant for a period of time as institutions transition toward compliance. For a comprehensive review by NAFSA of this matter, please refer to the most recent updates in the NAFSA Adviser's Manual 360 online (see http://www.nafsa.org/Content.aspx?id=26557).

Inventory of Types of IEPs in the United States

There is no standard IEP model, and the types of IEPs operating across the United States are notable for their diversity, although the Accreditation Act has had the effect of promoting greater commonality across the field. Programs vary due to geography as much as they vary by design, and the predominant factor determining the nature of an IEP is the student demographics they serve—and to what end.

Primary program models

- In-house college or university program—the IEP operates as a unit within an academic department of the institution, university extension, or as a direct report to an administrative department or executive.
- Partnership with third-party provider—the IEP is operated by an independent entity via a contractual relationship.
- Consultancy—a consulting entity assists the institution with the startup and/or development, management, and promotion of the IEP, which is the property of the institution.
- Stand-alone private institute—the IEP is managed by a private entity and operates apart from an academic institution.
- Multisite provider—the IEP is one of multiple IEPs in different locations managed by one private entity.

Program structure and length

Given the SEVP requirement for students on F-1 visas to remain "in status" throughout their course of study, an IEP must have the capability of providing instruction "full time" and through the academic year with the option of providing instruction during the summer (which most IEPs do.) The minimum number of hours of classroom instruction considered by SEVP to be "full time" is 18 clock hours per week, but some programs exceed this requirement by offering 20, 25, or even 30 clock hours per week. Program length is tied to the IEP's proficiency objectives typically expressed as "program completion"—the English proficiency represented by program completion varies widely depending on the nature of the program and thus program length and intensity likewise varies widely.

Decades ago, it was not unusual for a student to study for up to two years in an IEP, but over time demand has grown for expedited transitions from IEP into academic study to save time and money for students and their sponsors. In most cases, program structure is characterized by "multilevel" and "multiskill" offerings ranging from "beginner" to "advanced." Early examples of IEP program structure were developed in the 1960s at major academic institutions in the United States and the United Kingdom and propagated by the new professional association, TESOL, which was formed in 1966. The best practices of leading institutions were typically adapted to other institutions and private organizations over the decades. The TESOL Accreditation Advisory Committee developed agreed upon standards in the mid-1990s leading to the establishment of CEA and increasing consensus in the field.

Entry points and deadlines

IEP entry points do not necessarily have to align with a partner university's academic calendar and oftentimes points of entry are more frequent with mid-semester or mid-quarter admission points. Some programs have entry points each month of the year with little down time. There have been programs with weekly or biweekly entry points, though not widely utilized. When an IEP is housed on a campus, it is of course most advantageous to align entry points with the institution's start dates as much as possible to allow for easy transition of students from IEP into an academic course of study.

Categories of students/trainees served

IEPs may offer their instructional services to virtually any type of client of any age or background. U.S. citizens, permanent residents, refugees, tourists, dependents of nonimmigrants, and holders of certain types of visas may under certain circumstances study in an IEP part- or full-time. Most commonly, academic IEPs enroll students in their mid-teens and above and most of these students hold B-2, F-1, F-2, H-4, J-1, or M-1 visas or they are permanent residents or refugees.

Pros and cons of various models

It is worth noting that with so much variation, each program model has its pros and cons. With reference to the five primary program models mentioned earlier, a strong case can be made for each model under certain circumstances. The in-house institutional IEP ensures close alignment with the academic institution and quite often institutional IEPs have a built-in marketing advantage abroad being part of a university. The partnership with a third-party provider can be a win-win for both parties and offer unique flexibility and a range of services that other programs may not be able to match. Much depends on the mission and leadership of the institution in question as to which model is a better fit. Consultancy can provide a "best of both worlds" solution for some institutions; the risk is then entirely that of the academic institution as is the reward.

Stand-alone IEPs have great flexibility and naturally emphasize customer service and adaptability more than any other model. Multisite providers offer advantages in scale and geographic reach. They vary from having just a few sites to having hundreds of sites, and vary in the degree to which they can tailor their services to a particular location. There are very few private nonprofit multisite IEP providers and stand-alone IEPs, but they have a unique niche in their relationships with foreign government agencies, which frequently may be required to contract only with nonprofit entities.

Academic admissions screening criteria versus those essential to IEP admission

For the most part, IEPs are able to avoid requirements that are common to academic institutions such as minimum English proficiency, minimum GPA, completion of an educational program, references, and personal statements.

The essentials of IEP admissions processes

- **Criteria for admission:** (1) Demonstrated ability to make satisfactory progress in a full course of study, (2) ability to pay all required fees, and (3) minimum age (as determined by the IEP based on its accredited program plan);

- **Application form:** all versions now allowed including online apps;
- **Supporting documents:** (1) identity documentation, (2) evidence of financial support for SEVIS Form I-20 issuance, (3) evidence of insurance if opting out of institutional insurance plan;
- **English language proficiency screening/evaluation:** prescreening prior to arrival is not a requirement of most IEPs, but may be utilized to assist with planning for transitioning the new student into the program or into a pathway program; and
- **Transfer form:** form used to collect information necessary to accurately initiate a SEVIS transfer and assist with understanding the student's current level of English language proficiency based upon shared standards.

How can IEPs support academic admissions processes?

Established IEPs represent important know-how, historical, linguistic, and cultural knowledge, and detailed understanding of incoming students who are transitioning from IEPs. Overburdened admissions staff who may be relatively new to a campus or admissions department can take advantage of the expertise of those in the IEP to assist students and institutional staff and faculty. The IEP can provide critical value in the following areas:

- Setting college and university policies related to English language proficiency requirements: For decades, institutions have frequently held on to standardized test score requirements that were not based on empirical study of their effectiveness for that institution, but merely a matter of copying the practices of other institutions without regard for the effectiveness of that procedure. By partnering with IEP specialists, institutional decisionmakers can adjust their requirements to take advantage of changing demographics and more innovative educational models.

- Services to graduate teaching and research assistants: A major conundrum for many large research institutions is how to ensure that graduate teaching assistant (TAs) in particular have the necessary comprehensibility and competency in writing to function effectively. To ensure that non-native English-speaking TAs are supported in their transition into TA positions, IEPs can provide tailored solutions that non-specialists may find difficult to provide effectively.
- Multilingual, cross-cultural, and international expertise: It is easy to overlook the obvious fact that IEP administrators, instructors, and staff members often have a high degree of global competency that can be of great value to an institution seeking to internationalize further. These IEP employees and their volunteer support networks are crucial links to the community and to communities around the world and often represent a broader range of cultural knowledge than found in area-specific academic studies units.

Conclusion

In conclusion, the following are several key takeaways with regard to IEP admissions:

- The Accreditation Act of 2010 and the SEVP Conditional Admission Policy Guidance of 2013 were game changers for IEP admissions and operations in the United States and must be accommodated.
- IEP admissions procedures are relatively simple and can be easily tailored to align with academic institution realities within a short turn-around time because students do not have to plan ahead as they do for university; this means there are frequent last-minute applicants.
- IEPs offer a critical means of increasing enrollment overall by providing multiple entry points throughout the year and creating a backlog of students who are pre-oriented to a locale or an institution and require much less support on entry.

- Students are typically very diverse in age, ranging from middle school teenagers to older adults, and it's important to have this diversity to ensure there are enough students in an IEP to maintain a multilevel program year around.
- It is often easier for students to defer their start date to the next session or a later session of an IEP.

9 Resources for International Admissions Professionals

By Rachel Scholten

International admissions professionals wear many hats, serve many constituents, and work within many different types of office structures. Some work in large, comprehensive global affairs offices alongside immigration and education abroad advisers, some in small international units within a domestic admitting unit, others in stand-alone international admissions offices, and still others soldier along as an army of one.

Those who work in the field may serve international students at one particular academic level, many levels, or all levels. Some institutions perform all international credential evaluations in-house, while others choose to outsource this work to third-party organizations. Having an audience with such diverse needs and circumstances, it is important to keep in mind that not all of the resources discussed here will be the best fit for a particular office. However, it is the intent of this chapter to provide useful information that will be valuable and actionable to a wide variety of international admissions professionals.

Workshops and Networking

Working in international admissions requires a host of specialized knowledge and skill sets. Fittingly, there is a plethora of opportunities for training and professional development within the field. While it is beyond the scope of this chapter to review all available resources, what follows is a compilation of some of the most well established.

NAFSA's Core Education Program (CEP) workshops (see http://www.nafsa.org/workshops) cover a variety of topics and highlight best practices in international admissions. These highly structured workshops are designed to develop foundational knowledge and skills in international educators. Additionally, NAFSA's Current Topics Workshops (CTW) are often designed by members in response to emerging trends and needs. Both categories of workshops are routinely available at NAFSA's annual and regional conferences and locally via the On-Site Program. Other types of formalized training opportunities offered by NAFSA include e-Learning courses, e-Learning seminars, and NAFSA's Academy for International Education (see http://www.nafsa.org/Professional_Resources/Learning_and_Training/).

In terms of networking, NAFSA's Member Interest Groups (see http://www.nafsa.org/migs) and Knowledge Communities (see http://www.nafsa.org/kcs) provide excellent opportunities to learn from peer administrators and peer institutions. Member Interest Groups focus on particular types of institutions, such as community colleges or Historically Black College and Universities, while Knowledge Communities emphasize particular areas of international education, such as intensive English programming or international enrollment management.

The American Association of Collegiate Registrars and Admissions Officers (AACRAO) has a dedicated International Education Services branch (see http://www.aacrao.org/) that offers intensive, week-long trainings on international credential evaluation in its annual Summer Institute and Winter Institute events. These International Education Services workshops are located in Washington, D.C., where AACRAO is headquartered, and cover secondary and postsecondary credentials, transfer of academic credit, and the identification of fraudulent documents.

World Education Services, or WES (see http://www.wes.org/), puts on annual two-day International Credential Evaluation Labs with one day focusing on undergraduate credentials, and the other on graduate credentials. Past locations for these labs have included New York, San Francisco, and Toronto.

The Society for Intercultural Education, Training, and Research, also known as SIETAR (see http://www.sietarusa.org/), is a nongovernmental organization that connects professionals from a variety of industries who are interested in cross-cultural communication through its annual conference, mentorship program, and regionally based networks.

Conferences

In additional to NAFSA's (www.nafsa.org) annual conference and expo, the association also hosts state, regional, and multiregional conferences across the United States. These events provide great opportunities for networking with others working in the field of international education, as well as benchmarking against other institutions. There are also many opportunities from travel grants to volunteering typically available to eligible NAFSA members for reducing their cost of attendance.

The International Association for College Admission Counseling (International ACAC) hosts an annual conference that brings international admissions professionals together with college counselors from secondary schools around the world (see http://www.oacac.com/). The International ACAC conference is hosted by a different college or university each year. International ACAC also organizes regional college and university tours for international college counselors in collaboration with the participating schools, to allow them to experience the institutions firsthand and meet with the international admissions office members face-to-face.

The Washington International Education Council (WIEC) puts on a conference each year in Washington, D.C., which includes traditional conference seminars. It also organizes embassy visits that allow professionals from educational institutions to visit international government representatives directly (see http://washcouncil.org/).

The American International Recruitment Council (AIRC) hosts an annual conference (see http://www.airc-education.org/annual-conference) that brings together international admissions professionals and agencies from abroad and addresses topics related to international student recruitment and the use of educational agents.

The Association for International Credential Evaluation Professionals (TAICEP) organizes an annual conference focused on international credential evaluation and major trends impacting educational systems of the world.

Print Resources

The International Education Research Foundation (IERF) produces *The New Country Index* Volumes I and II, offering information and guidance on educational systems around the world, focused on such topics as secondary credentials, educational terms, and academic calendars and dates. *The New Country Index* Volumes I and II are available for purchase, while IERF's other publications can be requested free of charge (see http://www.ierf.org/for-institutions/ierf-publications/).

The Institute of International Education's (IIE) *Open Doors* report, issued each year, includes data on numbers of international students in the United States, their respective academic fields, levels of study, and countries of origin, and on top-receiving institutions of higher education (see http://www.iie.org/Research-and-Publications/Open-Doors). While some of the information is freely available online, a more detailed report can be purchased in print format.

The system of higher education in India, the second-largest source of international students in the United States, is particularly complex. The two-volume *Universities Handbook*, available through the Association of Indian Universities (see http://www.aiu.ac.in/publication/publication.asp), contains detailed and authoritative information on the complex system of affiliated colleges, deemed universities, and full universities operating within the Indian educational system. The *University Handbook* volumes do have separate prices in rupees and dollars, and are significantly cheaper in rupees, so institutions with offices or representatives based in India may benefit by making the purchase in-country.

Internet-based Resources

Credentials

NAFSA's Online Guide to Educational Systems Around the World (http://www.nafsa.org/ges) is a resource containing profiles of educational systems, credentials, and grading scales from around the world. Additional resources available from NAFSA include *Evaluating Foreign Educational Credentials: An Introductory Guide (2016),* a digital download available for purchase (see http://www.nafsa.org/pubs), the *IEM Spotlight* newsletter (see http://www.nafsa.org/iemspotlight), and chapter 6 of this book.

AACRAO owns and maintains the Electronic Database on Global Education (EDGE, see http://edge.aacrao.org/info.php#.WLcCAG_ysdU), a subscription service that provides research and recommendations for grading scales and credential equivalencies for nearly every educational system in the world. Each page on EDGE includes some background information on the country's system of education, and it drills down into detail when there are significantly different systems within a single country—for example, each province in Canada has its own dedicated entry.

WES hosts publically available information on country credentials and grading scales, as well as a Grade Point Average (GPA) calculator that can be used as an example of how WES would assess a GPA for a particular country and level of study. WES also offers frequent webinars, some free and some paid, on a variety of international educational systems, as well as publications on various topics in international education.

The National Collegiate Athletic Association (NCAA) publishes a document on international standards that is intended for use in determining academic eligibility of student-athletes who were educated outside the United States, but it can also serve as a resource on interpreting the U.S. equivalencies of international diplomas, certificates, and grading systems (see http://www.ncaapublications.com/).

It is not unusual to see dates from the Hijri calendar on transcripts or diplomas from predominantly Muslim countries; however, seeing the year 1437 on a recent document may give pause, and could cause issues if entered in a student information system. There are several online date calculators that can convert the Hijri month, day, and year and provide the corresponding date in the Gregorian calendar, including islamicity.com and islamicfinder.org. For institutions that accept the International English Language Testing System (IELTS) as evidence of English proficiency, the Test Report Forms can be verified online (see https://ielts.ucles.org.uk/ielts-trf/index.jsp).

News and Information Exchange

In the quickly changing field of international education, it is important to stay abreast of current trends—there are a variety of wonderful online resources to that end:

- *IEM Spotlight* newsletter (see www.nafsa.org/iemspotlight) is an online newsletter published three times each year by NAFSA's International Enrollment Management Knowledge Community. Each issue features a different country and offers insights related to the educational system, academic credentials, and enrollment trends.
- *ICEF Monitor* (see http://monitor.icef.com/) provides a wealth of information on markets in international education, best practices in the field, trends, and opinion pieces.
- The *Chronicle of Higher Education* (see http://chronicle.com/) and *Inside Higher Ed* (see https://www.insidehighered.com/) have discrete global sections for internationally themed current events, articles, and discussions.
- The *PIE News* (see http://thepienews.com/) is another great online resource that is specifically aimed at professionals working in international education jobs, and therefore puts out content that is especially relevant to those working in the field.
- World Education Services also publishes a monthly online newsletter, the *World Education News and Review* (see http://wenr.wes.org/), which can be subscribed to free of charge.
- International admissions professionals who wish to message prospective students or applicants abroad have many free options from which to choose. Skype (see https://www.skype.com/) is already a household name, and What's App (see https://www.whatsapp.com/), Viber (see http://www.viber.com/), and Kaokao Talk (see http://www.kakaotalkdownload.com/kakaotalk-features) offer similar, free, Internet-based voice and video calling, as well as instant messaging functions.

- Educational Credential Evaluators (ECE) hosts a free-to-join online platform called The Connection for International Credential Evaluation Professionals (see https://theconnection.ece.org/), which serves as a forum for questions, answers, and musings on specifics topics, documents, or qualifications related to educational systems worldwide.
- The United Nations Educational, Scientific, and Cultural Organization hosts a resource through its Institute for Statistics called the Global Flow of Tertiary-Level Students (see http://www.uis.unesco.org/Education/Pages/international-student-flow-viz.aspx). The web page includes downloadable data by country, along with an interactive data map allowing the user to sort the data by country to see where international students go to study, as well as their countries of origin.
- The World Bank also has a dedicated Tertiary Education section (see http://www.worldbank.org/en/topic/tertiaryeducation) with country-level data on a range of education-related indicators, including rates of literacy, enrollment, graduation, educational expenditures, and more.

Institutional Practices

While there are many external resources available to international admissions professionals, sometimes the best thing to do is to evaluate internal processes and make a plan to create one's own resources. Maintaining an internal database with information on institutional policies and procedures related to international admissions will help with preserving institutional memory, training new employees, and benchmarking against other institutions. The database could include samples of fraudulent materials, special cases, unusual credentials, preferred grading scales, international transfer credit procedures, processes for requesting and receiving final academic records, and so on. Additionally, whether an institution's admissions review processes are paper-based or electronic, creating a summary cover sheet for each file with the most salient information that will inform the admissions decision can help to streamline the review. This is especially helpful when files will be passed on to selective admitting units such as graduate academic departments or honors colleges that may not be familiar with international credentials, educational systems, and grading scales.

Finally, clear communication to both internal and external constituents on the required processes is essential. A web page with the required credentials for admission and expected minimum averages listed out by country can go a long way toward establishing accurate expectations as to the outcome of an application.

Core Qualifications for International Education Professionals

Attracting new employees with just the right qualifications and capabilities is essential in international education. Due to the complexity and uniqueness of international admissions work, it can be difficult to articulate exactly what skills are needed when there is a vacancy in the office, or when a new position is created. *NAFSA's International Education Professional Competencies*™ document is available free of charge (see http://www.nafsa.org/competencies). It identifies key strengths to look for in applicants, and suggests interview questions that can help hiring committees pinpoint these competencies in applicants.

The proposed qualifications that follow may also be helpful when it comes time to post a job opening, but it is important to keep in mind that needs will inevitably vary from institution to institution.

International admissions specialist/counselor/adviser

Experience working with diverse populations, exceptional customer service skills, strong cross-cultural communication abilities required, study or work abroad preferred, ability to represent the institution and its interests professionally to diverse groups of internal and external constituents, ability to triage workload and prioritize accordingly, willingness to work nights and weekends as needed.

International credential evaluator

Attention to detail, familiarity with complex and disparate international education systems, Chinese, Arabic, or Spanish language abilities preferred, meticulous nature, strong print-based and Internet-based research skills, ability to synthesize information from multiple sources and to perform evaluations in a consistent manner according to institutional policy.

Director of international admissions

Provide leadership to international admissions staff, create strategic international enrollment management plan, establish policies and best practices, maintain budget for staffing, office operations, and international recruitment, monitor return on investment for recruitment and yield initiatives, liaise with international student services and education abroad offices, provide guidance to university leadership on issues and new initiatives related to international admissions, advise university student services offices on unique needs of international groups, promote diversity, and advocate for international students on campus.

Government Resources

Certain country governments have created national strategies for international education initiatives within their borders, such as Canada (see http://international.gc.ca/global-markets-marches-mondiaux/education/strategy-strategie.aspx?lang=eng) and Australia (see https://internationaleducation.gov.au/International-network/Australia/InternationalStrategy/Pages/National-Strategy.aspx). These strategies may be able to point to additional resources, informative data, and sources of support for international admissions professionals. The Chinese Ministry of Education publishes lists of recognized universities, junior colleges, and adult colleges in spreadsheets in the English language on its government website (see http://www.moe.edu.cn/publicfiles/business/htmlfiles/moe/moe_2792/). Generally speaking, Ministry of Education websites are good places to search for information on institutional approval or accreditation in a given country.

EducationUSA (see https://educationusa.state.gov/) is a branch of the U.S. Department of State that provides college counseling abroad for international students who may not be familiar with the U.S. education system. EducationUSA offices can also be a great resource for international admissions professionals for country-specific questions, or when working with applicants from less commonly visited countries. There are now more than 30 U.S. international education consortia based on state or region that institutions can use as a resource and engage with, attending meetings or taking a leadership role and serving on the board. The list of current consortia, along with links to each individual consortium, is hosted by the International Trade Administration online at www.export.gov. The U.S. Department of Commerce (see http://2016.export.gov/industry/education/) also offers a variety of services designed to assist educational institutions in the recruitment of international students.

Additional Resources

In its online platform The Connection (see https://theconnection.ece.org), Educational Credential Evaluators (ECE) includes an article on how to build a library for an international admissions office that will serve as a continuing resource. NAFSA's Resource Library (see http://www.nafsa.org/resourcelibrary/default.aspx?catId=265) includes an International Enrollment Management (IEM) section with publications on a wide variety of IEM topics, as well as bibliographies that can point to additional resources. The National Association for College Admission Counseling (NACAC) has a webpage dedicated to resources for international admissions professionals (see https://www.nacacnet.org/knowledge-center/international).

Equipped with the knowledge of all of these resources, how does one sort through the options and determine which to pursue? A needs assessment can be a great starting point to determine what resources and knowledge already exist within a given office, and to identify areas where support is needed. Then, evaluate how much can be invested in new resources. If an office has limited funding, consider the free resources first. If there is a need for training, focus on the type of trainings that will provide ongoing support, or introduce a network that can be called upon in the future. When participating in one-time trainings, ensure that the information learned is share with colleagues, and that the presentation materials are saved for future reference in a way that can be accessed by all who may need it—for example, in an office shared drive. For offices that are committed to continuous professional development opportunities and ongoing training, consider starting a committee that can identify new avenues for growth, and organize officewide continuing education seminars.

There is no single magic bullet that will meet all of the needs of an office—offices grow and evolve, and the demands of the field of international education can change rapidly. If the services offered by a company or organization seem unclear, reach out to their representatives directly for clarification, consult with colleagues on their experiences using different materials, consider the options, and identify the best resources. International admissions professionals have a vast array of resources from which to choose—the trick will be to identify which may be the best fit, and to continuously assess and respond to new needs that arise.

References

Association of Indian Universities. 2014. *Universities Handbook (33rd edition).* New Delhi: Association of Indian Universities.

International Education Research Foundation, Inc. 2004. *The New Country Index: Making Sense of International Credentials.* Vol. 1. Berkeley, CA: Ten Speed Press.

International Education Research Foundation, Inc. 2010. *Index of Secondary Credentials.* Culver City, CA: International Education Research Foundation, Inc.

International Education Research Foundation, Inc. 2011. *The New Country Index: Making Sense of International Credentials.* Vol. 2. Berkeley, CA: Ten Speed Press.

International Education Research Foundation, Inc. 2012. *Index of Educational Terms.* Culver City, CA: International Education Research Foundation, Inc.

International Education Research Foundation, Inc. 2015. *Index of Academic Calendars & Dates.* Culver City, CA: International Education Research Foundation, Inc.

About the Authors

Peter Baker is EducationUSA's regional educational advising coordinator for western and northern Europe, based in Brussels, Belgium. Prior to his role at EducationUSA, Baker served as the first international program development officer at the University of Montana. In that capacity, he recruited and supported sponsored international students, designed and administered short-term programs for international students, and handled a variety of other projects. He holds a master's of teaching from Western New Mexico University's Peace Corps Fellows Program. He was a Presidential Management Fellow in the U.S. Department of Education's international programs office, and served as a Peace Corps volunteer in the Kyrgyz Republic.

Matthew Beatty directs international recruitment and admissions at Concordia College in Moorhead, Minnesota. He provides strategic leadership to the campus's enrollment and internationalization efforts. Beatty has a decade of practical experience in international recruitment, admissions, and student services. He completed his doctoral degree in educational policy and administration, with a focus on faculty engagement in comprehensive internationalization, from the University of Minnesota-Twin Cities. He received his bachelor's degree in Spanish language and literature from Luther College. Beatty is an active NAFSA member and chair-elect of NAFSA's International Enrollment Management Knowledge Community.

Blair Brown is director of international recruitment and retention at the University of North Carolina-Greensboro. In this capacity, he is directly responsible for increasing international student enrollment and retention for the university. Brown holds a BA in international relations with a concentration in western European politics from James Madison University, and an MEd in higher education policy from the University of Virginia. He is currently completing his PhD in higher education at the University of Virginia.

Grant M. Chapman is interim associate provost for international programs at Kansas State University (KSU). Prior to his role at KSU, Chapman held several faculty and administrative positions at Webster University, including associate vice president for academic affairs, director for international programs, and director of the London campus. Chapman holds juris doctor and master's degrees from St. Louis University and a bachelor's degree in political science from Oklahoma State University. He was a Fulbright Scholar on the International Education Administrators Program in Japan.

David L. Di Maria is associate provost for international programs at Montana State University, where he is responsible for advancing the international dimensions of learning, discovery, and engagement. He regularly presents, publishes, and consults on best practices pertaining to international education administration. Di Maria is a recipient of the NAFSA Region VI George E. Hertrich Advocacy Award, past-chair of NAFSA's International Enrollment Management Knowledge Community, and president of the American International Recruitment Council. He earned undergraduate and graduate degrees from the University of North Carolina at Greensboro and a doctorate from the University of Minnesota. His dissertation focused on campus services for international students.

Ryan Fleming is a client relations manager with IDP Education. His primary duties include business development, strategic enrollment planning with a focus on India, and contract management for the U.S. team. He obtained his master's degree in international affairs from The Pennsylvania State University in 2011 and his bachelor's degree in Spanish from SUNY Buffalo in 2009.

Mandy Hansen serves as senior international officer at the University of Colorado-Colorado Springs. She has worked in international education for more than 15 years. She has directed international admissions and recruitment, coordinated orientations, developed partnership programs, conducted grant writing and proposal writing, and advised international students and scholars. Hansen is an alumna of the Fulbright International Education Administrators Program in Germany and has served in leadership positions with organizations such as NAFSA and the National Association for College Admission Counseling. She received her doctoral degree at Northern Arizona University.

Lin Larson is senior assistant director/senior international specialist for the Office of Undergraduate Admissions at the University of California-Berkeley (UC Berkeley). She holds a BA in Asian studies from UC Berkeley. Larson has more than 17 years of experience working with international students. She held positions at Northern Arizona University and Saint Mary's College of California before joining UC Berkeley in 2010. As the international team leader, her duties include training application readers, mentoring colleagues, and advising students. Lin has presented on aspects of international student recruitment and admissions, credential evaluation, ethical practices, and institutional policies at several conferences, including NAFSA, American Association of Collegiate Registrars and Admissions Officers, and EducationUSA. She was instrumental in the MasterCard Foundation Scholars Program at UC Berkeley.

Ted R. McKown, II is the associate director of admissions at Kent State University. He has 24 years of experience in higher education administration. McKown completed his EdS in higher education administration at Kent State University, where his research focused on the academic integration of international students. He received a master's degree in counseling at Cairn University and a bachelor's degree in business administration and marketing from The University of Akron. McKown has held multiple leadership positions at the regional and national levels for NAFSA and the American Association of Collegiate Registrars and Admissions Officers.

Aleksander Morawski, director of evaluation services at Foreign Credits, Inc., is an experienced international enrollment management professional with an extensive background in credential evaluation, university admissions, and management. Morawski completed his bachelor's degree at Marquette University and master's degree at San Diego State University, both in political science with a focus on international relations. He is an active and experienced trainer and member of NAFSA Trainer Corps, presently serving as workshop dean of the credential evaluation curriculum. He has served as the NAFSA Admissions and Credential Evaluation network leader, and is a regular presenter at local, national, and international conferences.

Ujjaini Sahasrabudhe is the director of the Office of Graduate Admission at University of Southern California. She is responsible for coordinating with academic programs and managing graduate admission-related operations for the university. She holds master's degrees in human development and family studies, as well as social and multicultural foundations of education. Sahasrabudhe has presented at conferences such as NAFSA, Association for the Study of Higher Education, Comparative and International Education Society, NASPA: Student Affairs Administrators in Higher Education, and NAGAP, The Association for Graduate Enrollment Management. She also serves as the managing editor for NAFSA's *IEM Spotlight* e-newsletter.

Rachel Scholten serves as assistant director of international admissions at Fairleigh Dickinson University. Her current role involves recruitment, advising, communications, credential evaluation, and scholarship and admission decisions. She works with both international students and U.S. students abroad applying to all levels of study. Scholten earned a BA in sociology from the University of Pittsburgh and an MA in international development studies from Ohio University. She previously contributed a chapter to the NAFSA digital download *International Enrollment Management Strategic Planning: An Integrated Approach*, and has presented at regional, state, and annual NAFSA conferences.

Amy VanSurksum is associate dean of international student services at South Puget Sound Community College in Olympia, Washington, where she oversees international recruitment and admissions, international student services, and study abroad. She received her bachelor's degree in Russian studies and international relations from Concordia College, and her master's degree in cultural anthropology from North Dakota State University. VanSurksum has worked in international education at both the secondary and postsecondary levels since 1998. She has been an active NAFSA leader at the regional and national levels, in addition to serving as a NAFSA Academy coach and a member of the NAFSA Trainer Corps.

Jonathan (Jon) Weller is the director of international admissions at the University of Cincinnati (UC). He has helped develop and implement admissions policies and procedures, numerous international marketing and communication plans, and four international undergraduate scholarship programs. He is active in numerous professional organizations. Weller is also an adjunct instructor in the UC Department of Organizational Leadership, where he created and teaches the popular "How to Change the World" course and leads a study abroad program to Peru. He holds a PhD from the University of Cincinnati.

David B. Woodward is president of the American Consortium of Universities and principal for DAVID WOODWARD & ASSOCIATES LLC. Previously, Woodward served as president and chief executive officer of Associates in Cultural Exchange for 18 years. He holds master's degrees in higher education/TESOL and near eastern languages and civilization from the University of Washington. Woodward currently serves as the sponsored programs agency liaison of NAFSA's International Enrollment Management Knowledge Community and co-chair of NAFSA's Middle East Member Interest Group. He has held several volunteer leadership positions including chair of NAFSA's Region I, Commission on English Language Program Accreditation (CEA) commissioner, and local arrangements co-chair for the TESOL convention.

Index